Coaches give
How to Coach Little League Baseball
Two Thumbs Up!

**Straight shooting approach that
makes baseball fun again for the
players, coaches and the parents!**

Jake Patterson has been coaching youth athletics for over twenty years. He holds a Graduate Degree in Education and has a background in youth counseling. He has coached every level of baseball from Tee-Ball to high school and has published several books on coaching youth athletics. The book, *How to Coach Little League: A Short Easy to Follow Guide on How to Begin Your Little League Coaching Career* has been used at some of the largest coaching clinics in Northeast United States.

"Being the Webmaster of Baseball Almanac means I see a lot of coaching books over the course of a year. Jake Patterson's *How to Coach Little League* was easily the best of the lot during 2005. It was unique, informative, extremely valuable and easy enough to understand that I found myself in the back yard with Erika (My 9-year-old daughter who plays coach pitch) practicing actual techniques from the book minutes after I opened it."

- Sean Holtz, C.E.O. of Baseball Almanac, Inc.

"Great job on *How to Coach Little League Baseball.* It's the first easy reading instruction manual I found that helps me, the coach, deal with the not often talked about responsibilities of coaching youth athletics."

**-Ed Charlton, President, Thompson Little League
Thompson, CT**

"…The more information you get to the parents the fewer questions you have to answer during the season. Love the schedules and the letters home, great section."

**-Lisa Lindstrom., President and Coach, Woodstock Little League
Woodstock, CT**

How to Coach Little League Baseball

Second Edition
(2006)

Jake Patterson

To the many coaches who made youth baseball a special part of my life and to the young players that have made coaching a wonderful experience for me. Also, to Dad and JD who always had time to play catch.

Acknowledgements

First and foremost, I would like to thank *you,* the volunteer coach. Without you the Little League memories and dreams of many children would not be possible.

Jake Patterson

Former Little League Coach

SECOND EDITION
(February 2006)

*"It was so long ago, I don't remember how many games we
won or lost that year….*

….but I do remember my dad coaching."

Table of Contents

Introduction

Becoming a coach is one of the most rewarding and enjoyable experiences you will ever have. It is extremely important to the children you coach to be the best possible coach you can be. This can only be accomplished one way. *LEARN!* There are two quotes that have guided me throughout my coaching career. They are:

> *"He who dares to teach must never cease to learn."*

And

> *"The measure of a good coach is not how well he knows the game, it's how well he can teach it."*

There are many great books, videos and clinics available to the volunteer coach. The Little League sponsors a great education program for coaches. You can obtain further information by contacting the Little League at:

Little League Eastern Regional Headquarters

PO Box 2926
Bristol, CT 06011
Telephone: 860-585-4730
Fax: 860-585-4734
Email: *eastregion@littleleague.org*

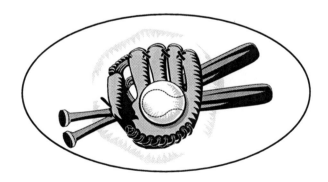

The Purpose of This Book

The purpose of this book is to provide you, the Little League coach, with an easy-to-read guide to assist you throughout your season. Please bear in mind I do not profess to know everything there is to know about the game of baseball and softball. I have found, like many things in life, that the more I learn, the more I realize how much there is to learn.

"The future Little League memories of our children are being made today."

- Jake Patterson

Section 1. The Little League Coach

The Little League Coach's Job

1. YOUR MISSION AS A COACH

Coaching Little League can be a very rewarding experience. It is very important however, that you keep a proper perspective of what your priorities and mission should be at this level of competition. Your primary responsibility is <u>NOT</u> to win! The pressure of winning will come soon enough for these young athletes. Your primary mission as a Little League coach is to:

Unfortunately, many coaches live their adult athletic lives through their young players. Visions of days gone by cloud their judgment, and teaching and developing young players takes a back seat to their own personal athletic gratification. While your personal experience, as a *former* player will be very important throughout your coaching career, it is imperative to remember that you are no longer a player, you are a coach. Knowing how to do something is much different than knowing how to teach it. The later being a much more difficult endeavor.

2. YOUR RESPONSIBILITIES AS A COACH

It is important to remember that your players look up to you. You set the example. You should always act like a coach when on the field and be aware of your actions when you are off the field.

Other responsibilities include:
     a. Safety.
     b. Learning the game.
     c. Being polite, kind and approachable.

d. Being fair by providing ALL players the opportunity to learn.
e. Making every player feel they are a part of the team regardless of their talent level.
f. Dressing like, and looking like a coach.
g. Setting reasonable goals and expectations.
h. Teaching the fundamentals of the game.
i. Being positive no matter what the outcome.
j. Knowing and supporting Little League Baseball and Softball rules and programs.
k. Being honest and not afraid of admitting your own mistakes.
l. Being open-minded.
m. Being a role model for the children.
n. Understanding that growth and progress come one small step at a time.
o. NEVER yelling at a child.
p. Setting rules and following them (See Rules section).
q. And remembering the game is *for the children.*

3. SUCCESSFUL COACHING

Determining whether or not you were successful at the end of the season is not as difficult as some may think, and it does not only include your win/loss record. Evaluating your success at the youth level can be determined by asking yourself the following questions:

a. Was I able to get the absolute best out of the athletes?
b. Did I leave the athletes feeling more confident about themselves as people, and more confident in their abilities as athletes?
c. Did they enjoy themselves, and did they feel comfortable being an active member of the team?
d. Did they excel in the concept of good sportsmanship and treating opponents, teammates, fans and officials politely?
e. Did they learn the skills we taught them?
f. Did I leave them a little more prepared for life's challenges?

4. ESTABLISHING YOUR TEAM PHILOSOPHY

Every coach is different and therefore his or her philosophies will vary. There are however, basic expectations that should be required from the players. Establishing how you are going to run the team and informing the players and parents on the first day is important for a successful season. Your team philosophy should include:

a. Be the absolute best you can be at every practice and game.
b. Improve in your skills through practice.
c. Work hard at becoming physically fit.
d. Learn as much as you can about the game.
e. Always support the team and your teammates.

f. Always conduct yourself in a respectful manner and represent the town and your team with pride.

5. *TEAM RULES*

Team rules allow you run the team effectively and efficiently. They insure every participant gets the most they can from the Little League experience by preventing the waste of the team's most precious resource; *time*. The following items should be reviewed with both players and parents at the beginning of each season:

a. When the coach speaks everyone listens.
b. When you do not understand something, ask questions.
c. Stay focused.
d. Always use good sportsmanship.
e. Follow instructions.
f. No one leaves the field until all the equipment is stored and the field and dugouts are clean. I sometimes tell the players, "I'm your coach, not your maid." Their mess, their responsibility.
g. Whistle blows, everyone stops.
h. When on the bench always yell encouragement, never yell instructions or criticism.
i. Always work hard.
j. Learn the game.
k. No horseplay.
l. No one starts practice until the coach arrives.

Johnny Unitas

Many years ago I had the privilege of meeting one of America's greatest athletes, Johnny Unitas. Johnny and I were paired off as partners in a golf tournament. During the match I found that Johnny was one of the most unpretentious guys I have ever met and we quickly fell into, "a bunch of regular guys just playing golf and talking routine." I asked Johnny: "What was the most rewarding part of your career?" He replied without batting an eye, "Teaching kids football. Of all the things I accomplished, I enjoyed coaching kids the best."

---

6.   *THE QUESTION OF WINNING VERSUS TEACHING AND DEVELOPING*

Winning is a hotly debated topic in youth sports. Many sports psychiatrists feel that we have gone too far, placing too much emphasis on winning. We developed the following table several years ago with the help of college and professional coaches, and a sports psychologist. It may help address your questions concerning this subject.

Table 1.1: Winning Versus Teaching and Developing

Categories	Category 1	Category 2	Category 3	Category 4	Category 5
Coaches' Emphasis	*WIN*	*WIN / DEVELOP*	*WIN / TEACH / DEVELOP*	*DEVELOP / TEACH / WIN*	*TEACH*
Description	Primary function is to WIN at all costs. Jobs are on the line.	Primary function is to win while further developing. Athlete is looking at playing at a higher level.	Primary function is to teach the finer points of the game. Winning IS becoming a priority.	Athlete has a basic knowledge of the game. Teaching and developing is the key. Winning is NOT the priority.	Athlete has little to no knowledge of the game. WINNING and LOSING does not matter. Teaching the game to all members of the team is the priority.
Team Types Level	Professionals College Olympic Team National Teams	College Semi-Pro's Olympic Development Teams	High School American Legion Babe Ruth Little League All-Stars	High School JV High School Freshman Middle School Junior League Senior League	Tee Ball Minor League **Little League** Recreation Leagues
Typical Age Group	Adults	Young Adults	Teenagers (15-18)	Teenagers (12-15)	5-12 Year Olds
Type of Training	Training is very hard and vigorous. Those that can't keep up are cut. Athletes are selected based on their talent. Expectation to win is very high.	Training is hard and vigorous with emphasis on development. Athlete knows the game and is expected to develop the finer points.	Training is somewhat hard. Teaching is still a key coaching priority.	Training is NOT hard and somewhat fun. Coach is teaching and developing the athlete by improving basic skills. Coach's primary job is to prepare the athlete for a good season of play. Player effort should be rewarded with playtime regardless of skill.	Training is FUN and fast moving (game-like). Coach's only concern is teaching the game. Everyone should have an EQUAL opportunity to play.
Commitment	Work is year-round. Hard work	Seasonal Hard Work, year round conditioning.	Work is seasonal. Athletes typically play other sports.	Seasonal and fun. Athletes sometimes play other sports.	Seasonal and always fun.
Fun Factor (1= Hard Work, 10= Fun Play)	1	2	3	7	10

7. TRYOUTS

Conducting tryouts is a very difficult process for a coach. Deciding who plays and who does not, always results in broken hearts. While most Little Leagues provides guidelines for this process, there are those instances where tryouts are necessary. Middle School teams, AAU teams, and other non Little League teams can be used as examples. Keep in mind that most Little Leagues are able to accommodate all players that want to play. Those players that don't make a Little League team are usually assigned to Minor League team.

There are several guidelines that can make the tryout or assignment process easier.

a. Establish standards prior to the tryouts. Ask yourself, "What are the criteria I will use to select my players?" Avoid, at all costs the, "*I know a good player when I see him,*" approach. The good players will not be your problem.

b. Communicate your standards via written letter to both parents and players. Ask the parents to review the standards with their child at home. This helps both the parent and the player understand what is expected and helps prepare the child for their big day.

c. Do not allow parents on the field where tryouts are being conducted, unless they are part of the coaching staff. It is unfair to both their child and to the other players.

d. Review the tryout schedule and expectations with the players on the first day. Tell them what you will be looking for and when you expect to make your cuts.

e. Plan for players that either cannot make tryouts or who are sick. The options of how to handle this can range from special tryouts to no show/no play. The key is to be prepared.

8. TRYOUT LETTER

The following is an example of a tryout letter I use. Please note, this letter would be appropriate for players trying out on a school team and would have to be modified and adjusted for the level you coach. It is best to get this letter out during a parent/player meeting prior to tryouts. If this is not possible then I would suggest handing them out the first day of the tryouts.

Babson Tigers Baseball Tryouts

What To Expect And, What Is Expected

First and foremost welcome to the 2006 baseball tryouts. The reason for tryouts is simple; we have more players trying out than there are team positions. If you do not make the team and want to play DON'T get discouraged. KEEP PLAYING! The town has a great Little League program.

We've listed three areas we are looking for during tryouts. Please remember that a spot on last year's team doesn't necessarily mean an automatic place on this year's team. We expect returning players to work as hard as new players.

What we're looking for:

#1.) ATTITUDE: Our coaching and playing philosophies puts attitude as the key ingredient for having a successful team. We would rather work with a player with a good work ethic and attitude than a person with exceptional skills that demonstrates poor sportsmanship and is not willing to learn. Baseball is a team sport.

#2.) ABILITY: There are six key areas that you will be rated on. They are:

1. **Long and Short Distance Running:** This gives us an idea of your speed, and endurance, both essential elements of the game.
2. **Catching**
3. **Throwing**
4. **Hitting**
5. **Overall Knowledge of the Game**

#3.) POTENTIAL: Athletes develop at different rates. Some players demonstrate marginal abilities but have exceptional talent. We will be looking at potential for future school teams. This category however, will not count as much as attitude and abilities.

IF YOU HAVE QUESTIONS PLEASE ASK!

Coach Patterson
pattersonsports@yahoo.com

9. *TRYOUT TALLY SHEET*

To keep tryouts as fair as possible, it is necessary to develop measurable criteria. Do not go into tryouts with preconceived notions on the player's ability. Players develop at different rates and there are always those that will surprise you.

I use a simple system that has helped me greatly over the years. Bear in mind it is not the most talented players or the least talented players that present the challenge when selecting your squad, the challenge usually lies in selecting those players from the middle of the group. Having quantitative data helps. The following is an example of a tryout sheet. You may have to adjust it to better fit your particular needs.

Table 1.2: Tryout Tally Sheet

Item	Player 1 Name:	Player 2 Name:	Player 3 Name:	Player 4 Name:	Player 5 Name:	Etc
RUNNING						
Long Distance Running						
Shuffle Step						
Cross Step						
Back Step						
Base Running Speed						
FIELDING THROWING						
Ground Balls						
Fly Balls						
Throwing						
HITTING						
Hitting						
Bunting						
OVERALL						
Attitude						
Potential						
TOTAL						
RANKING						

I usually conduct school tryouts for three days, with the first cut being made on day two. This gives me ample time to observe the player's skills and abilities, and it gives the players time to relax and demonstrate to the coaching staff what they can do. Little League tryouts are usually held on one day, requiring heavy preparation from both the coaches and the players.

When ranking the players I issue a tryout sheet to all my assistant coaches. They are each tasked with scoring the player's skills on their own. These sheets are kept with the coach and are not reviewed with other coaches or players. Upon completion of the tryouts the coaches meet to discuss their findings. Once the decision of who stays and who gets cut is made, the sheets are destroyed and are not discussed with players or parents. I will not answer the question, "Why did he make the team and I didn't?" I will however, always take the time to answer the question, "What do I need to work on in order to make the team next year?"

The scoring system I use is fairly simple and can be modified to suit your individual needs. The scores are posted to each individual item and tallied at the end of the tryouts. The top scores make the team. The scoring I use is as follows:

Table 1.3: Tryout Scoring

Points Awarded	Criteria
3	Player exhibits excellent mastery of this skill for this age group.
2	Player exhibits basic skills for this age group and can become proficient with further training.
1	Player exhibits fair skill level for this age group and is trainable.
0	Player does not exhibit skills required for this level. Further development will be needed before playing at this level.

10. A WORD ABOUT ATTITUDE AND POTENTIAL

As coaches we must recognize that attitude and potential are important elements when selecting a team. I always reserve the right to award points to marginal players because they exhibit exceptional attitude and potential. While these two elements are important, I do not rank them above abilities. I will use them as a tiebreaker for the last few positions.

11. THOUGHTS ABOUT TRYOUTS AND YOUR CHILD

Having tryouts with your own child as a participant can be difficult. Drawing the lines as to what is fair for your child and what is fair to other children is not always easy. There are several reasonable guidelines I use that have helped me through this very difficult issue. They are:

a. *Paid Position.* If you are a paid coach, you have the responsibility to be fair to all children who participate. These positions are usually school teams. Your child needs to be placed on the tryout squad with everyone else and they need to make the team on their own abilities. Here, you are paid to do a job and are expected to do it well.

10

b.   *Volunteer Position.* Examples of volunteer positions include Little League, recreation leagues, Pop Warner Football, etc. Here you are a volunteer and you volunteer because of your child. I have always felt that certain latitude should be given to the children of those willing to give their time. This does not mean however, that your child should be given special treatment once the teams are established and tryouts completed.

c.   *All Star Teams.* Many coaches that do well during their regular seasons are asked to become part of the All Star team coaching staff; this is especially true in Little League. In this case your child should not be afforded special privileges. An All Star team represents the league you belong to and must be made up of the league's best players. Most league volunteers have children that play, not all are good players. If your child makes the team fine, if not, you will have to decide whether or not you can coach the team without your child. I used my son as a team manager one year and he loved it.

12.   *THOUGHTS ON PLAY TIME*

Table 1.1 hopefully places some perspective to the topic of winning. Winning is important in athletics. We don't play to lose and I am not a big proponent of the, "Let's not keep score," mentality, except at the Tee-Ball level. Children learn from winning, losing and playing. The lessons they learn however are up to us as parents and coaches.

There are numerous books written by experts that explore the need for social acceptance, and a sense of belonging in children. I won't even attempt to go there. The important thing is to recognize that a sense of belonging is critical to proper child development. Many young athletes are made, or more importantly broken, by insensitive coaches that lose track of individual playtime, or lack thereof. The Little League has guidelines for substitution and playtime. Remember they are only guidelines and represent the *minimum* amount of time each player should play.

Another important item here is that most coach-parent arguments are due to playtime. Parents hate to see their children sit the bench and become angry when it happens too often. Many headaches can be avoided by managing individual playtime well. Here are several guidelines I use when coaching children.

Table 1.4: Playtime Guidelines

Level	Typical Age	Items to Consider
Junior League Senior League Middle School Varsity AAU Travel Teams Little League All Stars	12-16	1. Start your best players. 2. Establish a role for everyone on the team, i.e. back-up infielder, reliever, pinch runner, etc. 3. Try players at different positions during practices and regular season games. 4. Include everyone during huddles. 5. In games that are clearly won or lost use everyone on the bench 6. Rotate bench players so that the same players do not sit game after game. 7. When ever possible, play everyone.
Little League (Regular Season) Minor League Tee-Ball Town Recreation Leagues Church Leagues	12 and under	1. Rotate starters. Give everyone a chance to shine during the regular season. 2. Everyone plays. Stay away from token playtime (See article on Token Playtime). 3. Allow players to play various positions. 4. Include everyone during huddles.

Remember, the Little League also has guidelines concerning the amount of playtime each player should receive per game. Keep in mind these are minimum guidelines and may not necessarily represent the *right* amount of time for each of your players.

13.   ROLES AND RESPONSIBILITIES

Well-established roles and responsibilities can be an important element to a successful season. These roles include the head coach, assistant coach, team captain, manager and players, and in some cases, a team mom or dad. This section will explain these roles and their associated responsibilities.

It is important to note that I am not suggesting you utilize each of these roles for every youth team. Every team's needs are different and younger children may not possess the skills necessary for the job of team captain or manager. I usually recommend using the roles of team captain and manager at the middle school, high school, Junior League, Senior League, AAU, and American Legion levels.

The following is and overview of each role and the associated responsibilities.

Table 1.5. Roles and Responsibilities

Position	Overview	Responsibilities
HEAD COACH	The head coach has the ultimate responsibility for the team and team activities. He/she is responsible for the overall development of the team and insuring every player has a positive experience.	1. Season master schedule 2. Daily practices schedules 3. Team's Mission Statement 4. Establish team line-up 5. Discipline and counseling
ASSISTANT COACH	The Assistant coach is there to assist the head coach. They do not make teams decisions or create situations that are in conflict with the head coach. They work at the discretion of the head coach.	1. Assist with practices 2. Advises head coach of problem areas. 3. Learn specific functions assigned by the head coach such as hitting coach, pitching coach, etc. 4. Perform duties required by the head coach. 5. Learn the game. 6. Fills in for the head coach when necessary. 7. Supports the head coach with parent conflicts.
TEAM CAPTAIN	Being selected Team Captain is an honor. Coaches and players recognize the Team Captain as a leader on the team. Their main responsibilities include leading warm-ups, exercises, and performing other job functions deemed necessary by the head coach. It is important to note that the position of team captain is a position of responsibility, NOT a position of authority. Team captains are part of the team and NOT part of the coaching staff. **Team Captain Selection Process:** Selection can be made in one of three ways: 1. Coaches select captains based individual performance and leadership ability. 2. Players select captains based on individual performance and leadership ability by voting. 3. Combination of 1 and 2.	**A Team Captain:** 1. Shows up early for practice to assist with equipment set up. 2. Secures equipment after practice or game. 3. Helps insure all players have proper equipment. 4. Notifies coaches of problem areas. 5. Notifies coaches of potential safety problems. 6. Leads warm-ups and exercises. 7. Motivates through example. 8. Assists teammates with problem areas 9. Learns each position to the best of their ability. 10. Insure team integrity is maintained by including all players in all activities. 11. Assists with maintaining field after practices and games. 12. Assists with pre-season field clean up and the development of an, "our field, our job" mentality. 13. Insures uniforms are properly worn. 14. Insures dugouts and buses are cleaned after a game or practice.

TEAM MANAGER	Team Manager's primary responsibility is team statistics, books and records. They assist with administrative duties assigned by the head coach. The position is an appointed position that reports directly to the head coach. Team managers are selected based on their ability to perform the necessary assignments. Managers must have a good working knowledge of baseball statistics.	Team manger Is responsible for scorebooks and team and individual statistics. They include: 1. Batting averages 2. Hitting percentages 3. Slugging percentage 4. Stolen bases 5. RBI 6. ERA's 7. Pitch counts Other responsibilities can include: **Pre game:** 1. Notify the coach if the team needs water. 2. Insure game balls are available. 3. Insure medical kit is in the dugout and available. 4. Report any absences (if known) to coach. **Pre game (Book):** 1. Obtain starting lineup from head coach and neatly fill in scorebook, lineup card, and umpire's card. 2. Insure all player numbers, playing positions and batting positions are accurate, reporting any problems to the head coach. 3. Obtain starting lineup from opponents and insure both scorebooks agree. **During the game:** 1. Keep the book tracking strikes, balls, hits, errors, stolen bases, RBI's etc. 2. Stay available to coaches for lineup questions. 3. Inform players of the batting order at the beginning of every inning. 4. Insure the batters hit in sequence announcing the next on-deck batter. 5. Inform coaches of opponent's previous at bats. 6. Insure all substitutions are recorded properly and insure players are aware of all changes. 7. Inform opponents of changes. 8. Cross check scorebook with other team after the second, fourth and sixth innings to insure they agree. 9. Insure the umpire's count is well kept reporting any problems to the head coach.

		After the Game:
		1. Insure the book is complete and ready for statistical analysis.
		2. Report scores and highlights to school for school Website and/or newsletter.

Keep in mind the above are guidelines only. You need to adjust the roles and responsibilities you use based on your team's specific needs.

14.   *RUNNING UP THE SCORE – WHEN IS ENOUGH, ENOUGH*

We have all heard the stories of coaches that have gone too far with score management. Unfortunately, games of 15-0 are not uncommon in all levels of baseball. I have even witnessed a game with a score of 23-0, and that game was called in the fifth inning because the league utilized a mercy rule. These games are going to happen; how you manage this type of game is extremely important for the players on both teams. An easy way to avoid doing the wrong thing is to ask yourself the question, "What are the children, on both teams learning?"

While there are considerable dynamics working in such a lopsided game, one thing is certain - the children learn little when playing a game like this, if it remains unmanaged. An unmanaged game is defined as a game where the winning coach does little to control the game and his/her intent is to run the score up.

On the other hand, regardless of the score, I have never told a player to strike out, make an error, or blow a play intentionally. There are many ways to curb a large score differential while still winning or losing a game. There are several guidelines I have used over the years that may be helpful. They are:

Table 1.6: Lopsided Games

League Level	Score	Items to Consider During a Lopsided The Game
Tee Ball	Score is not a priority.	1. Make sure everyone plays everywhere. 2. Move players around each inning. 3. Do not allow players or parents to emphasize score. 4. These games are strictly for fun and learning.
Minor League	League playoffs make score somewhat important.	1. The intent of Minor League is still to learn. 2. Make sure everyone plays everywhere. 3. Put bench players in early. 4. Try new pitchers.

Little League	Playoffs make score important.	1. Make sure everyone plays everywhere. 2. Put the bench players in early. 3. Use different players at different positions. 4. Try different pitchers. 5. Avoid stealing for the sake of stealing. 6. Hold runners from taking extra bases. 7. Avoid bunting on weak defenses. 8. Avoid using better pitchers when not necessary.
Little League All Stars	Winning is the priority	1. Use bench players early. 2. Use relievers early. 3. Avoid stealing for the sake of stealing. 4. Hold runners from taking extra bases. 5. Avoid bunting on weak defenses. 6. Try new pitchers.
Junior League, Senior League	Playoffs make score important.	1. Use bench players early. 2. Use relievers early. 3. Avoid stealing for the sake of stealing. 4. Hold runners from taking extra bases. 5. Avoid bunting on weak defenses. 6. Try new pitchers.
Junior League, Senior League All Stars	Winning is the priority.	1. Use bench players early. 2. Use relievers early. 3. Avoid stealing for the sake of stealing. 4. Hold runners from taking extra bases. 5. Avoid bunting on weak defenses. 6. Avoid using better pitchers when not necessary.
Middle School Varsity	Winning is the priority	1. Use bench players early. 2. Use relievers early. 3. Avoid stealing for the sake of stealing. 4. Hold runners from taking extra bases. 5. Avoid bunting on weak defenses. 6. Avoid using better pitchers when not necessary.
High School Junior Varsity	Playoffs make score important.	1. Use bench players early. 2. Use relievers early. 3. Avoid stealing for the sake of stealing. 4. Hold runners from taking extra bases. 5. Avoid bunting on weak defenses. 6. Avoid using better pitchers when not necessary. 7. Try new pitchers.
High School	Winning is the priority Note: Possible college careers may hang in the balance. This does not however, override your responsibility to the game and all the players.	1. Use bench players early. 2. Use relievers early. 3. Avoid stealing for the sake of stealing. 4. Hold runners from taking extra bases. 5. Avoid bunting on weak defenses. 6. Avoid using better pitchers when not necessary. Note: the level of pitcher you use controls many of these games.

Both coaches also need to use common sense here, even the losing coach. I have had games where, when up a considerable amount of runs, I replaced all my starters with bench players in an effort to make the game better for both teams. The losing coach seeing an opportunity began a relentless pounding on my inexperienced bench players. This resulted in me re-entering my starters when there was only a one run difference, sealing the other team's fate. I was not about to lose a game we were easily winning.

In another incident I had a coach have his players steal third and home when he had a fifteen run lead in the top of the last inning. I had already burned through, my now completely demoralized pitching staff and there was no hope for us winning the game. I quietly asked him to ease up, to which he replied, "Welcome to the big leagues coach." His comment epitomizes how some coach's view coaching young players; they think they're coaching in the big leagues.

Most of the lopsided games I have witnessed or have participated in during my career occurred simply because one team dominated the other team, this will inevitably happen during each season. Most coaches do the right thing. I have however, seen those coaches that will simply run the score up. They accomplish little more than placating their own egos. Players, on both teams, learn little during an unmanaged lopsided game. Again, the best way to avoid this is to ask yourself the question, "What are the players on both team learning?" Most of all remember, they're just kids.

Section 2: The Legal Responsibilities of The Coach

Legal Responsibilities of the Coach

The legal liability associated with coaching is the most significant reason many states, leagues, and school districts are certifying and formally training their coaches. Our litigious society has made everyone paranoid about getting sued. First and foremost, don't be frightened by this process. If you use common sense you should never have a legal issue. Each state is slightly different with regards to the legal requirements of coaching, but if you keep the following in mind, you should never have an issue.

1. *LEGAL DUTIES OF A COACH*
   a. Provide adequate supervision for your players. Do not allow them to practice on their own unsupervised. Do not allow the players to continue to play after practice is finished. You are responsible for them until their parents pick them up.
   b. Provide sound planning and preparation (See section on practice schedules).
   c. Warn players of inherent safety risks (See safety section).
   d. Provide a safe environment (See safety section).
   e. Evaluate and accommodate any athlete's disabilities. An example of this would be resting an asthmatic player that is having difficulty breathing.
   f. Match and equate your players. Pair off players based on their skill level and size. Avoid having new players playing the corners, first or third during batting practice.
   g. Be able to provide emergency first aid. Always have a first aid kit available.
   h. Provide emergency communications in the event of an accident or injury.

2. *ADDITIONAL RESPONSIBILITIES*
   In addition to the above, the coach must also provide the following:
   a. You must assure that the basic civil rights of the players are not violated. This includes derogatory comments.
   b. You must consider the spectators as well as the players. Unfortunately, you share some responsibility for the players' parents and family.
   c. Keep good records, particularly in the event of an injury. Document each accident listing the type of injury, care provided, time of accident, reason for injury, witnesses, etc.

Bear in mind I do not profess to be a legal expert. If you have legal questions you should seek the advise of a lawyer. Many leagues have counsel available to them.

Section 3. Safety

Baseball Safety

Player safety is a key responsibility of all coaches and parents. The following is a list of items that should be reviewed with the players during the first practice and always be considered when practicing and playing.

1. *BATS*
   a. Always swing the bat in control. Use the, "Double Distance" rule. Players with bats must be more than two bat lengths away from the next closest player.
   b. Drop the bat. Never throw it.
   c. Always wear a helmet during live batting practice.
   d. Use the right size bat (See hitting section).
   e. Make sure the bat grips are in good condition.
   f. Make sure the bats are well cared for and are not damaged.

2. *BALLS*
   a. Always have players throw in control.
   b. Always have players face the ball during batting practice.
   c. Ensure players face the ball and present a target when throwing.
   d. Do not use damaged or wet baseballs. Note: Practicing in the spring will inevitably result in wet baseballs. I have salvaged many wet baseballs by placing them in the oven at 150° F for a half hour or so.

3. *EQUIPMENT*
   a. Ensure all male catchers wear cups
   b. Encourage all male players to wear athletic supporters
   c. Ensure catchers wear their full equipment including shin guards, mask, cups, helmet, and chest protector.
   d. Clips *OUT* on shin guards. Clips in will get caught and trip the player.
   e. Ensure players wear proper footwear. Many leagues have restrictions and guidelines for approved footwear.

4. *FIELD*
   a. Walk the field prior to every practice and game. Look for problem areas such as holes, damaged fences, loose bags, etc.
   b. Have players report all problems or potential safety hazards with the field to the coaches immediately.
   c. Ensure all players are aware of the fences and gates.
   d. Keep fingers inside the dugout! A line drive hitting a finger grasping a chain link fence is very painful.

5.   *OTHER*

    a.   Perform dynamic stretching before every game and practice (See Warming Up The Athlete).

    b.   Perform static stretching after every game and practice (See Warming up the Athlete).

    c.   Ensure players who wear eyeglasses wear athletic eyeglasses or eyeglasses with straps.

    d.   Prevent heat exhaustion and cramps by providing water and water breaks before, during, and after the games or practices.

    e.   Ensure the players pay attention and never clown around.

    f.   Have players avoid heavy meals before games or practices.

    g.   Have players inform the coach immediately if they are sick. Don't play players who are ill, no matter how much they are needed.

    h.   Bandage all cuts and be aware of blood-borne pathogens. Always use disposable gloves when bandaging an injury.

    i.   Report all injuries to the league and parents if they are not in attendance. Follow-up with a phone call that day. Keep good records on injuries to players.

    j.   Never allow players to move anyone who is hurt.

    k.   Never allow players to start the practice without the coach being present.

    l.   When in doubt as to the seriousness of the injury, call 911. Always err on the side of caution.

    m.   The Little League also has guidelines for blunt force chest injuries. Make sure you understand what is required of the coach when a player sustains a blunt force chest injury.

Section 4. Parents

Parents and Sports

Parents can present the most difficult challenge to you as a coach. We have all heard the stories of parents whose inappropriate behavior have ruined youth sporting events. Many organizations and leagues have incorporated a *Parent's Code of Ethics* in an attempt to help with this quickly growing problem. I use the following Code of Ethics when the league does not provide one. I have the parents sign it at the beginning of the season.

1. PARENTS' CODE OF ETHICS

Parents' Code of Ethics

1. *I will always remember the game is for my child, not for me.*
2. *I will respect all participants and spectators no matter what their race, creed or ability.*
3. *I will always remain positive with my child and his teammates.*
4. *I will not shout instructions to my child from the sidelines.*
5. *I understand the responsibility of instructing my child during games and practices belongs to the coach.*
6. *I will always encourage good sportsmanship and fair play.*
7. *I will hold all my input, comments, and criticism for the coach or officials until after the game or practice and will present it in a positive manner away from the players.*
8. *I will not interfere with practices or games.*
9. *I will insist that my child play in a safe and healthy environment.*
10. *I will insure my child is properly equipped.*
11. *I will support the umpires and other league officials.*
12. *I will always get my child to practice on time and pick him or her up on time and I acknowledge the coach is not a babysitter.*
13. *I will require the league provide appropriate training for the coach and his or her staff.*
14. *I will demand a drug, alcohol, and tobacco free environment and I will refrain from their use at all youth sports events.*
15. *I will do my very best to make youth sports fun for my child.*

---

2. *OTHER ITEMS*

Other helpful guidelines concerning parents are:

   a. Establish yourself and your coaching philosophies at the beginning of each season. Send team letters home at the beginning of the season listing expectations of both the players and parents.

   b. Don't avoid parents, even the troublesome ones. (See section on Problem Parents). Always speak to them when they want to talk with you. Ask them however, to wait until after the practice or game.

   c. Avoid talking to the parents about playing time and position assignments.

   d. If parents have suggestions or comments, listen to them and let them know you will consider their input.

   e. Avoid speaking with parents if you or they are angry.

   f. Set rules with the parents. They can include:

      1. If they have something to say, have them wait until after the practice or game.

      2. Ask them *NEVER* to shout instructions to the players as it may conflict with what you are telling the players from the bench. This will lead to confusion, which leads to player frustration.

      3. Ask them to always cheer in a positive manner. This means a lot to the players.

      4. Remind them, their job is to take pressure *OFF* their child not put it *ON*.

      5. Ask them never to yell or argue with the umpires. This sets a bad example for the children and detracts from the learning potential.

      6. Ask them to be on time when dropping off and picking up their children. Make sure they understand you are not a babysitter. You should however, do your part by starting on time and finishing practices on time.

   g. Be careful about choosing who assists you with coaching and managing the team. Good intentioned parents that know little about the game can become a training distraction.

   h. *REMEMBER*, you are a parent. You need to be fair with your own child. Most coaches tend to be very hard on their own children, ruining the Little League experience for them.

3. *DIFFERENT TYPES OF PROBLEM PARENTS*

During my coaching career I have participated in a number of coaches' clinics. At the end of numerous clinics, the coaches were asked to describe their number one challenge as a volunteer coach. Each time the answer was the same; PARENTS!

Some parents present the biggest challenge you may face as a coach. I have encountered several types of problem parents over the years and found each requires a somewhat different approach when addressing. The key is, don't avoid problem parents. They won't go away. The following are several types of problem parents, their identifiers and suggestions on how to handle them.

Table 4.1: Problem Parents

Problem Parent Type	Identifiers	Suggestions
The Expert	• Provides unsolicited advice. • Interrupts practices and games with, "helpful hints." • Makes, "If I were you" statements. • Contradicts or disagrees openly with your teaching methods.	• Be open-minded. Many of these parents have good input and they really do know what they are talking about. • Don't dismiss advice that may help you and the team. • Use the "Hear, Understand, Appreciate, Consider, Follow Up" approach (see below). • You may want to consider using this parent as an assistant. • Tell the parent to hold all input until after the practice or game.
Second Guesser	• Second-guesses coaching decisions and discusses with everyone except you. • Makes comments like "We could have won that game if he pitched Bobby! What was he thinking?" • Rolls his/her eyes and makes it known he/she does not agree with your line-ups or batting orders.	• Take the parent aside after the game. Tell him/her you understand he/she has concerns and you would like to talk about them openly. • Inform the parent that second-guessing the coach's decisions with players and other parents brings little value to the process. • Set up a time with the parent to discuss his/her concerns. • Use the, "Hear, Understand, Appreciate, Consider, Follow Up" approach (See below).

Disruptive Influence 	• Interrupts practices and games with silly reasons. • Sticks their head in the dugout to see, "How things are going." • Distracts the players. "Hey Bobby! Keep your hands up!" • Asks during a game "Hey Coach! Why isn't Bobby playing shortstop?" • Embarrasses themselves and their children. • Makes inappropriate remarks to players, coaches, officials and fans. • Usually has a negative tone.	• Address this problem immediately! The longer you wait the worse the problem becomes. • Be polite; speak with the parent after the game. "Hey Mr. Smith would you mind hanging around for a few minutes after the game? I have something to discuss with you." • Inform the parent the team would be better served if all comments were kept on a positive basis during and after the game. • A videotaped recording may enable the parent to better understand his/her actions. • If the parent continues to misbehave schedule a meeting with league officials to solicit their help. Some leagues have specific protocols established. • If the parent continues to be a disruptive influence, inform the parent you may be forced to remove his/her child from the team. • In extreme situations where the parent is totally out of control, and you cannot continue the game peacefully, call the police and have the parent removed.
Never Gets Involved 	• Never commits to help. • Provides little to no support. • Loner.	• An important fact to remember when dealing with Little League parents is that many parents simply do not know how they can help or what they should do. It is as new to them as it is for their children. • Take the initiative and introduce yourself and ask, "Would you like to help with the team? There's so much to do and I could use all the help I can get." • These parents sometimes make great team moms or dads.

Never Satisfied 	• Everything is a problem. "Why do we have to sell candy? I gave you my money at registration!" "Why aren't there enough Porta Potties?" • They complain about everything.	• Speak with them after the game or practice. • Ask them what it is they would like to see done. • Ask the parent how he/she would resolve the issue. • If the issue is a team related item, use the, "Hear, Understand, Appreciate, Consider, Follow Up" approach (See below). • If the issue is not team related, i.e. field condition, fundraisers, schedules etc., ask the parent to help organize a solution. • These parents sometimes make great team moms or dads.
Irresponsible 	• Always late • Forgetful • Unorganized	• Meet with the parent after a game or practice. • Tell the parent, "Bobby could get so much more out of the game if you could get him here on time." • If this does not work, tell the parent, "I take what I do seriously. To make the experience great for everyone, you need to do your part." • I have even had to tell a parent once that their child will have to be removed from the squad because of their inability to get their child to practice on time and pick them up on time. • Have the parent make alternative arrangements.

Most of all don't blame the kids!

4. *HEAR, UNDERSTAND, APPRECIATE, CONSIDER, FOLLOW UP APPROACH*

Problematic parents come with the territory. Few coaches go through their seasons, let alone their entire coaching careers without having an issue with parents. Each coach needs to develop an effective and comfortable way to handle problem parents. Everyone is different and therefore his or her solutions and methods will also be different. Over the years I have developed my own style on handling problem parents. I call it the Hear, Understand, Appreciate, Consider, Follow up Approach. It is simply telling the parent:

"I *HEAR* what you are saying.

I *UNDERSTAND* your concern, and

I really *APPRECIATE* your input.

I will *CONSIDER* it carefully, and

I will *FOLLOW UP* with you later."

The following would be a typical sequence of events concerning this approach.

a. A parent approaches you during a game or practice with comments, advice or complaints.

b. If it does not concern an imminent safety problem tell the parent you really want to hear what he or she has to say. I would suggest saying, "Would you mind hanging around after the game (or practice) so I can give you my undivided attention."

c. As soon as the post-game meeting or practice is finished, meet with the parent somewhere private.

d. Listen intently to what he or she has to say and avoid impulsive comments or arguing. Always remember, what the parent has to say may be helpful.

e. Tell the parent, "I hear what you are saying, I understand your concern, and I really appreciate your input. I will consider it carefully and I will follow up with you later."

f. Establish a follow up date and time.

Using the above approach has helped me through many difficult situations. It has also allowed me to learn new things that I might not have had the opportunity to learn. This approach gives the parents a chance to voice their concerns. It also forces you to listen to what they have to say and gives you the time necessary to properly evaluate their input.

5. LETTERS TO THE PARENTS AND PLAYERS

The following are examples of parent letters I have used in the past. You may need to modify them to accommodate your particular philosophies, training methods, and circumstances. The first letter establishes who you are and what your background is. This helps introduce you and your assistant coaches to the parents and players.

6. INTRODUCTION LETTER

Babson Tigers' Baseball

Introduction Letter

Dear Parents,

   I am very excited about this season. This year we have Fred Smith joining the coaching staff. Fred is no stranger to baseball. He is known in this area as one of the best players ever to come from our local high school. He played college ball at McWilliam's College. He continued his baseball career as an assistant coach at Babson High School. During the day, Fred is a Service Manager for Moon Beam Electronics.

   This is my tenth year coaching baseball. I have a M.S. Degree in education and teach here at Patterson Middle School. I am also a State Certified Coach and have attended and organized many coaching clinics.

   I was never known as a good player myself, but I played tenaciously and made up for my lack of skills with hustle. Over the last ten years I have coached every level of players from beginners to high school and enjoy coaching more than playing.

   Our coaching philosophies are very basic. We feel there are six factors that have made us successful as coaches. They are:

1. We were able to get the absolute best out of the players.
2. We left the athletes feeling more confident about themselves as individuals and they developed more confidence in their abilities as athletes.
3. The players became, enjoyed and were comfortable being active members of the team.
4. The players excelled in the concept of sportsmanship and treating everyone politely.
5. The players learned the basic skills they were taught throughout the season.
6. We left the players a little more prepared for life's challenges

   You will not hear us berating the players about winning. We feel that everyone who puts on a uniform, wears a glove or picks up a ball doesn't do so to lose. We believe in the basics, teamwork and sportsmanship. We will work hard for the athletes and expect hard work from them. We will listen to them when they need help. We will also listen to you, the parents, when you have suggestions and comments. We ask however, that you hold these comments or suggestions until after the games or practices away from the players. We also ask that you encourage and cheer for the team when they are playing. <u>DO NOT</u> yell instructions. They may be in conflict with the instructions they are getting from the coaches. We won't entertain the question from either the athlete or the parent "Why am I not playing much and (so-and-so) is?" We will however, ALWAYS answer the question, "What do I need to do to improve my game?" We feel this to be fairer to the athletes and their teammates.

Again, we are very excited about this season. If you have any questions, please call me at 800-555-1234 or contact me at: pattersonsports@yahoo.com

_____
Jake Patterson
Head Coach

_____
Fred Smith
Coach

7. PHILOSOPHY LETTER

The following letter helps establish your team philosophy. It helps the athlete understand what you expect from them. Each team may have a slightly different letter based on the level of players you coach. The following letter would be considered appropriate for Little League, middle school, Junior League, Senior League and high school ball.

Babson Tigers Baseball

2004 Team Philosophy

Baseball is a team sport. One player not playing to their potential during the game can mean the difference between a great game, and a not so great game, no matter how hard the other players are playing. It is the responsibility of every player on the team to:

- Be the absolute best you can be at every practice and game.

- Improve in your skills through practice.

- Work hard at becoming physically fit.

- Learn as much as you can about the game.

- Always support the team and your teammates.

- Always conduct yourself in a respectful manner and represent the town

  with pride.

If you dedicate yourself to the above, success will follow. The desire to win goes without saying. We will always play to win the game. Remember however, improvement and sportsmanship are just as important as winning a game.

_____
Coach Patterson
pattersonsports@yahoo.com

8. *RULES AND REGULATIONS*

A letter sent to each player and parent stating team rules will help you manage your team effectively and efficiently. Keep in mind that many parents and players are first-time participants in the Little League experience. They may not understand what is expected of them. The following is an example of a letter I use at the middle school and high school level and can be easily modified for Little League.

2004 Babson Tigers' Baseball

Rules and Regulations

Absences:
- You are expected to make every practice on time. If you cannot make the practice or games or expect to be late, it is your responsibility to notify the coach. Unexcused practices may result in, "bench time."

Conduct:
- All players must adhere to the following, "Code of Conduct."
  1. No team member will use foul language at any time.
  2. No horseplay or fighting at any time.
  3. You will treat everyone with respect. This includes your teammates, coaches, referees, opponents, and fans.

Uniforms:
- The uniform will be worn properly.
- Shirts will be tucked in. Hat visor forward.
- Uniforms will be clean for each game.
- The full uniform will be worn during pre-game warm ups, unless the head coach allows something different.

Playing Time:
- No one is guaranteed a starting or permanent position. Players will be selected based on their abilities, performance and attitude during practices and games.

Away Games:
- All players are required to ride the bus to and from the game. No player may ride home with another player without a note from the parent. Each player is required to dress appropriately for away games.

Drugs / Alcohol / Smoking:
- Any one caught with drugs, alcohol, cigarettes or any other banned substance will be disciplined in accordance with League or school policy.

Schoolwork:
- <u>Schoolwork comes first!</u> Notify the coach if you are having problems or need extra time or help with schoolwork.

Drop Off and Pick Up:
- It is your parent's responsibility to insure you are picked up and dropped off on time. You must make alternative plans if your parents cannot pick you up on time. Students cannot be left alone at the school.

_____

Coach Patterson
pattersonsports@yahoo.com

9.   TEAM MOM OR DAD

Something you should consider at the beginning of each season is recruiting a team mom or dad. There will be many parents who know nothing about baseball, softball, or the art of coaching, but they are very willing to help the team with planning, transportation, scheduling, and team refreshments. Inevitably you will have fundraisers, team parties, and cash collections that will detract greatly from what you do best, coach. Recruiting a team mom or dad to handle these tasks will take a huge burden off the head coach and the assistant coaches.

Section 5. Warming up and Exercise

Warming up the Players

An essential part to every practice is properly warming up the players. Playing without warming up the players is unsafe and *will* lead to injuries. A common mistake made by many Little League baseball and softball coaches is allowing players to play catch in order to warm up. Do not let players throw before they stretch and exercise. It's very important to remember:

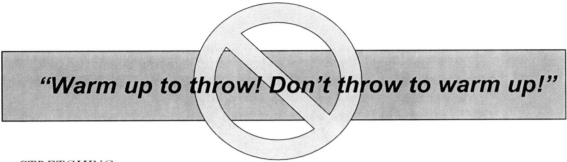

"Warm up to throw! Don't throw to warm up!"

1. *STRETCHING*
    Proper stretching is important for a successful practice. It helps by:
    1. Increasing the pulse rate, which provides a maximum oxygen supply to the body.
    2. Eliminating waste products from the muscles.
    3. Increasing the blood flow to the muscles.
    4. Increasing muscle temperature, which allows for improved performance.
    5. Preventing injury.

2. *HOW TO CONDUCT PROPER STRETCHING*
    There are two types of stretching, dynamic and static. Static stretching is conducted on a single plane, and gradually lengthens one muscle or muscle group at a time. Dynamic stretching occurs in multiple planes and gradually lengthens more than one muscle group at a time.

3. *DYNAMIC STRETCHING*
    Dynamic stretching helps muscles prepare for movement. Good Little League dynamic stretching can include:
    a. Light jog around the field
    b. Lumber jacks – Start with the glove in both hands up in front, on the right side above the head. The player moves the glove down to the left hip, lifting the right leg, knee to waist height. Perform 10-15 repetitions and then change sides. This can also be done starting out in front of the shoulder moving down to the outside of the opposite ankle.

c. Trunk twists – Hold the glove both hands out in front of the body, forearms parallel to the ground, one hand on either side of the glove. Twist right, back to center. Twist left, back to center. Perform 10-15 repetitions.

d. Butt kicks – Players run in place kicking the back of their thighs below the butt.

e. Arm circles – Place arms straight out to the side. Players rotate their arms in large circles for 15-20 seconds, and then reverse direction.

f. Squat thrusts – Place arms straight out, player squats in place. Perform 10-15 repetitions.

g. Crab walks – Players on all fours, inverted, butt down. Have them walk approximately thirty feet, and then reverse direction.

h. High skips – Exaggerated arm swings while skipping across the field. Have the players reach out as far as they can with each skip. The knees are brought up to the belt.

i. Sliding jumping jacks – Player performs jumping jacks while side stepping across the field. Have players perform exaggerated arm swings on top as well as in front of their bodies.

j. Combination run drill – Sprint to first base, side step to second base, cross step to third base, back step home. Run twice and reverse direction.

k. Finger squeezes – Hands straight out and in front of the body. Players quickly squeeze fingers into a fist for one hundred cycles.

You should always insure the athletes break a light sweat while performing dynamic stretching. All throwing drills should be conducted *after* the players perform dynamic stretching and some running.

4. *STATIC STRETCHING*

There are more than twenty static stretches recommended by most stretching professionals. They include stretches to the neck, arms, hands, legs, hamstrings, and ankles. I would recommend the book, *Stretching* by Bob Anderson, ISBN #0-936070-01-3. Static stretching can be done before and after the game or practice or if an athlete is injured.

Remember !

"Warm up to throw!
Don't throw to warm up!"

Table 5.1: Basic Little League stretches

Sitting butterfly – Elbows inside the knee	Inverted hands over the head	Behind the head arm
One leg extended	Lean back arm and leg	Over the head upper body
Calf muscle - against a wall	Leg up- on the back	Lay flat on the back
On the floor inverted hands	Lean forward legs out	Sitting leg lift

The above are basic stretches that should be done at every practice. All are bi-lateral and should be done with both sides of the body. Remember if it hurts – don't do it!

Section 6. Practices

How to Conduct a Successful Practice

When organizing your practice it's important to remember children get bored very fast! Come to practice prepared. Establishing a good practice schedule only takes a few minutes and will make your practice much more successful and enjoyable for the children.

1. *PRACTICE CONSIDERATIONS*

There are several key considerations when establishing your practice schedule. They are:

a. Age appropriate practice times. Not all age groups should practice the same amount of time. Younger children get little out of the experience when practices are too long. Use the following as a guide for maximum practice times.

Table 6.1: Suggested Practice Times

Level	Age	Suggested Time in Minutes (Hours)	
Tee-Ball	5-6	60	(1)
Minor League,	7-10	60 – 90	(1-1.5)
Little League	10-12	90	(1.5)
Junior League, Senior League, Middle School	13-16	90-120	(1.5 – 2)
High School	15-18	120-180	(2 – 2.5)

b. Practices should begin with dynamic stretching and running. Make sure the players have broken a light sweat before proceeding with the practice.

c. Practices should always include throwing and catching drills.

d. You should review your last practice and today's practice with the players at the beginning of each practice. Ask the question, "What did we learn yesterday?" Followed by, "OK, here's what we're going to be doing today."

e. Teach a new skill at every practice.

f. Have a game-like component at the end of each practice.

g. Keep the players constantly moving by having 7-8 different activities planned.

h. Avoid line drills. When necessary use your assistant coaches and keep everyone moving!

i. Start with the basics and work up. Use a building block approach.

2. *ITEMS THAT HELP DURING A PRACTICE*

Utilizing a whistle during practice helps eliminate confusion and makes your practice more effective. Many coaches are reluctant to use a whistle. The whistle can be the coach's most effective weapon in maintaining order and control. Other items that help are:

a. Use cones. They are inexpensive and will help save a tremendous amount of time by eliminating confusion. Kids can easily see a line created by using two cones; they cannot see the imaginary line made by the sweep of a hand. Cones are readily available at stores like K-Mart and Wal-Mart.

b. Set up stations using assistant coaches. Have assistant coaches come to practice a few minutes early in order to review their responsibilities for the day's instruction.

c. Use batting cages when available. Make sure however, that the coaches are properly trained in how to use the cage effectively.

d. Use a white board to explain new concepts. Children are visual and do their best when they can see what you are teaching.

e. When using a pitching machine, insure it is properly set. Coaches should be trained in proper loading techniques in order to best simulate real pitching. If using a pitching machine, set prior to practice. They can sometimes take a while to set up. A whole book could be dedicated to this topic so ensure your coaches are well versed in proper usage.

f. Always use your best throwing coach during batting practice.

3. *PRACTICE SHEDULES*

I cannot stress the importance of practice schedules enough. They only take a few minutes to develop and they save an incredible amount of time and energy in the long run. They are key in helping the coach establish credibility with players and parents. Even coaches that have never coached before can be effective if they are organized and well prepared.

Several important thoughts about practices and practice schedules include:

a. Use a building block approach when teaching young players. It is best you assume they know nothing about the game. Do not take the simple things for granted. How many of us have seen a young batter run the wrong way after hitting the ball, or stand in the batters box after being called out on strikes? Our job as coaches is to ensure that all players know the basics.

b. Plan your season by establishing a pre-season master schedule. The master schedule helps establish a balanced perspective to the season and keeps you on track. It is a "living" document that provides organization to the season. Specific master schedule items are similar for every level. The speed in which you can cover those items however, varies depending upon the level of the players you coach.

c. When conducting drills, use a whistle and stop watch and make a game of every drill. Tracking players' performance helps them to understand the desired standards and their relative position and improvements to those standards.

The following is an example of a master schedule and individual practices for the first six days. You may have to adjust them to suit your team's needs. Don't worry about whether or not they are perfect. Having a less than perfect written schedule is always better than a perfect schedule in your head. If your schedule is not written down you will get easily distracted and become inefficient with your practice time.

4. MASTER SCHEDULE

BABSON TIGERS
BASEBALL
Master Schedule

Each coach should establish a master schedule at the start of each season. The master schedule is a list of basic skills that need to be taught and/or reviewed throughout the season. Utilizing the building block approach, the skills should start with the basics and move to the more complicated tasks as players develop. There are two safe assumptions when establishing the master schedule. First, every team and every player is different. The timeline and lesson intensity will also be different. Second, children and their bodies forget! Baseball/softball skills require a great deal of muscle memory. Start with the basics every season.

The following is a suggested, "building blocks" Master Schedule for Little League:

Table 6.2: Master Schedule

Day	Topic	Item
1	Team rules and expectations	Team rules and expectations Team philosophy Your expectations of the parents Safety Proper practice dress and equipment
1	Baseball/softball field and terms	Field review and playing positions Baseball/softball terms Rules of the game
1	Warming up	Dynamic stretching Static stretching Exercise Running
2	Throwing instruction	Proper grip (4-seam versus 2-seam) Throwing techniques
2	Catching instruction	Base - Ready position Upper body Hands (M's and W's) Proper techniques in playing catch
3	The Glove	How to size How to wear How to properly maintain and break in a glove How to play catch with the glove

3	Catching drills	One handed self toss – Proper grip location Short toss - (no glove) Short toss - (glove) Ground ball basics Ground ball circle drill (tap/pass) Ground ball circle drill (gloves) Ground ball line drills, coach toss Fly ball Fly ball drills 3-man relay drill
4	Hitting	The bat (How to size) Proper grip Stance (Base) Head and eyes Upper body Stride and separation Swing and finish
5	Base running	Primary, secondary leads Slide and cross step Base returns Home to first First to second Second to third Third to home
	Other items	Pitching The catcher Field positions Game like situations Proper tagging techniques Run down drills and techniques Passed ball drills Relays Cut-offs Dead ball drills Offensive bunt work Defensive bunt work Bare hand drills Backing up the bags and plate Double plays Outfield ground balls (Outfield fence drills) First and third drills Tagging Bunting Ground ball blocks Sliding techniques and drills Pre-game routines Throw-downs Squeeze plays Etc.

There are literally thousands of drills that can help your players. You need to develop drills that best suit your team. The Little League, professional clinics, local high school and middle school coaches, the Internet, your local library and the American Baseball Coaches' Association are all great resources.

Table 6.3: Defensive Positions and Field Numbers

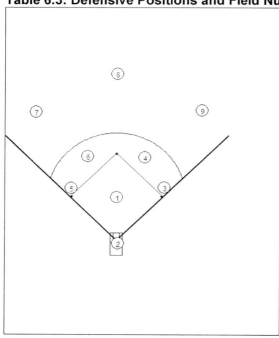

DEFENSIVE POSITIONS AND FIELD NUMBERS

The following are the numbers used for each position.

1. Pitcher
2. Catcher
3. First Base
4. Second Base
5. Third Base
6. Shortstop
7. Left Field
8. Center Field
9. Right Field

10. Extra Fielder (Used only in Softball)

The above is covered during your first practice. I still find it amazing how many children at the Little League level do not know the above. This is simply because they were never taught.

5. *PRACTICE SCHEDULE DAY 1*

BABSON TIGERS
BASEBALL

Today's Emphasis: GETTING STARTED   Date: *DAY 1*

Item	Time	Coach	Item	Comment

1.	10 Mins.	H/C	Introductions:
			   a. Players
			   b. Coaches
				See LL Manual

2.	5 Mins.	H/C	Team Rules: Cover how to dress and what equipment to bring to each practice.	See LL Manual
3.	5 Mins.	H/C	Safety	See LL Manual

4.	30 Mins.	Assnt.	Review the playing field:
			   a. Dugout (why it's there and proper behavior while in the dugout).
			   b. Boundaries (Fences, backstops, etc.)
			   c. Foul lines
			   d. Outfield fences
			   e. Batter's Box
			   f. Mound
			   g. Bases
			   h. Bullpen
			   i. Playing positions
				Don't take anything for granted.
				Walk players around the field.
				Make a game of it. Call a spot and have them run to it.

5.	15 Mins.	Assnt.	Basic rules and terms of baseball:
			   a. Hits, fouls
			   b. Infield hits
			   c. Outfield hits
			   d. Ground balls, pop-ups, line drives
			   e. Strikes and balls (Strike zone)
			   f. Double plays
			   g. Slides, steals
				Demonstrate

6.	15 Mins.	H/C	Warming up and stretching:
			   a. Dynamic stretching
			   b. Exercise
				"Warm up to throw. Don't throw to warm up!"

7.	10 Mins.	H/C	Review:
			   a. Review practice.
			   b. Questions?
			   c. Review expectation letters for parents.
				Have letters available for parents.

Coaching Notes:
   a. The first practice sets the stage for the entire season. Be prepared, look like a coach and act like a coach.
   b. Have fun with the kids and make a game out of today's topics.
   c. Send the parent letters home with the players. This is important to do on the first day. Most problems with parents can be avoided by communicating your requirements early.

6.   *PRACTICE SCHEDULE DAY 2*

BABSON TIGERS
BASEBALL

Today's Emphasis: THROWING AND CATCHING   Date: *DAY 2*

Item	Time	Coach	Item	Comment

1.	10 Mins.	H/C	Review last practice:
			  a. Team rules
			  b. Safety rules
			  c. Review playing field
			  d. Basic rules and terms
			  e. Etc.
				See yesterday's schedule

2.	15 Mins.	Assnt.	Warming up – stretching	See LL Manual

3.	20 Mins.	H/C	Throwing Class:
			  a. Grip (Teach/demonstrate/practice)
			  b. Proper grip. 4-Seam – 2-seam (How to use the "C")
			  c. "Butterfly" technique
			  d. Bow and arrow technique
			  e. Fingers on top
			  f. Cross body throw
			  g. Teach/demonstrate/practice
			  h. Pocket finish
			  i. Practice short toss drill
				Use tennis balls or "Incredaballs."
				
				See LL Manual.

4.	25 Mins.	H/C	Catching class (Start with no glove)
			  a. Body position and stance
			  b. Proper target, "M's and W's"
			  c. Receiving the throws
			  d. Practice / drills
				See LL Manual and handouts.

5.	10 Mins.	Assnt.	Play short toss. No glove – correct problems	Coaches pair off. One coach one side, one coach on the other side. Use cones to establish lines.
6.	10 Mins.	H/C	Review practice	Ask questions. What did you learn today?

Coaching Notes:
  a. Throwing/catching is a critical skill. If the team is having trouble ask for help, use different drills.
  b. First day of throwing/catching can be intimidating use tennis balls they are similar in size.
  c. Concentrates on the basics- keep it simple!
  d. Make all the drills fun. Keep them moving and avoid line drills
  e. Keep in mind that some young players at the Tee-Ball level do not know if they are right handed or left handed. They may need some help here.

7. *PRACTICE SCHEDULE DAY 3*

BABSON TIGERS
BASEBALL

Today's Emphasis: THROWING AND CATCHING DRILLS   Date: *DAY 3*

Item	Time	Coach	Item	Comment

1.	5 Mins.	H/C	Review last practice
			  a. Throwing
			  b. Catching (No glove)
			  c. Review how to play catch
				See yesterday's schedule

2.	10 Mins.	Assnt.	Warming up and stretching	LL manual
3.	5 Mins.	Assnt.	One handed self-toss. Check for grip	

3.	5 Mins.	H/C	Class on the baseball glove:
			  a. Different types and how to use and wear
			  b. How to take care of the glove
			  c. How to size
				LL manual

4.	10 Mins.	Assnt.	Short toss (no glove):
			  a. Short toss – sit throw
			  b. Short toss - kneel throw
			  c. Check for hand positions and throwing techniques M's and W's
			  d. Check for consistent presentation of a target
			  e. Short toss (glove)
				Players having problems should be taken aside. Use assistant coaches.

6.	15 Mins.	H/C	Ground ball class:
			  a. Review proper "set, ready" position
			  b. Alligator catching (Clam-shell catch)
			  c. Button to button drill
				Tennis balls

7.	15 Mins.	Assnt.	Ground ball drills:
			  a. Coach toss one line
			  b. Two line player toss
			  c. Small ground ball circle drill (no glove)
			  d. Small ground ball circle drill (glove)
				As your season progresses you should increase the difficulty of these drills.

8.	10 Mins.	H/C	Fly ball class:
			  a. "Ball" drill – Calling for the ball
			  b. Catching the ball out front
			  c. Drop step spot drills	

9.	10 Mins.		Fly ball drill:
			  a. "Easy fly"
			  b. "No look fly-ball" drill"
			  c. "To and away" drill	

10.	5 Mins.	H/C	Review	
Coaching Notes: The intent today is to teach the players the basic techniques and drills. This will help facilitate future practices.				

8. *PRACTICE SCHEDULE DAY 4*

BABSON TIGERS
BASEBALL

Today's Emphasis: BATTING AND HITTING   Date: *DAY 4*

Item	Time	Coach	Item	Comment
1.	5 Mins.	H/C	Review last practice	See yesterday's schedule
2.	10 Mins.	Assnt.	Warming up and stretching	LL Manual
3.	30 Mins.	H/C	Drills: a. Short toss (no glove) b. Short toss (glove) c. Small ground ball circle drill (no glove) d. Small ground ball circle drill (glove) e. Fly ball drills f. 3-Man relay drill g. Ground ball sequence drills	Keep these drills moving.
4.	20 Mins.	H/C	Hitting class: a. The bat (How to size) b. Grip c. Stance (Base) d. Head (Eyes) e. Upper body f. Stride and separation g. Swing h. Safety first!	LL Manual
5.	20 Mins.	Assnt.	Drills: a. Shoulder to shoulder drills b. Slap the monkey c. Small bat drills d.	All coaches should be coaching here. Use several stations and keep batters moving. Teach fielders while hitting.
6.	5 Mins.	H/C	Review	

Coaching Notes:
  a. Tell players if they have a bat in their hands they must be wearing a helmet.
  b. Double distance drill. Two bat rule.
  c. Limit batter to cycles of 10 hits.
  d. The players are better off going through limited hits, multiple cycles.
  e. 7-10 seconds between pitches. Let the batter reset and have a coach correct problem areas.
Take problem batters aside for additional help. Be aware not to waste the time of many players for the sake of one.

NOTES:

9. PRACTICE SCHEDULE DAY 5

BABSON TIGERS BASEBALL

Today's Emphasis: RUNNING THE BASES   Date: *DAY 5*

Item	Time	Coach	Item	Comment
1.	5 Mins.	H/C	Review last practice	See yesterday's schedule
2.	10 Mins.	Assnt.	Warming up and stretching	LL Manual
3.	25 Mins.	H/C	Catching – throwing drills: a. 2-man short toss (no glove) b. 2-man short toss (glove) c. Ground ball sequence drill d. Ground ball circle drill e. Fly ball drill f. No look fly ball drill g. No look ground ball h. 3-man relay i. Long toss	Start mixing up these drills. Make them fun. Time the drills and have the players compete against each other and themselves. Give them expectations for each drill i.e.: 3-cycles of 3-man relay in 30 seconds.
4.	25 Mins	Assnt.	Hitting drills: a. Tee drills b. Swing drills c. Hitting (Batting practice)	Set up stations. Use every coach.
5.	20 Mins.	H/C	Base running: a. Side step / cross step b. Basic running techniques (what to look for) c. First base running – 3 options d. Second base e. Third base f. Running drills	See Running Section.
6.	5 Mins.	H/C	Review	

Coaching Notes:
a.   Don't overestimate the player's knowledge of base running. This is an important aspect of the game.
b.   Be creative on drills. Establish names for each, so players will recognize them by week two.
c.   Teach them to look for a fielding error on first base. It's a basic of the game that often gets ignored.

NOTES:

10. *PRACTICE SCHEDULE DAY 6*

BABSON TIGERS
BASEBALL

Today's Emphasis: PULLING IT TOGETHER   Date: *DAY 6*

Item	Time	Coach	Item	Comment
1.	5 Mins.	H/C	Review last practice	See yesterday's schedule
2.	10 Mins.	Assnt.	Warming up and stretching	LL manual
3.	20 Mins.	H/C	Catching –throwing drills: a. Short toss (no glove / glove) b. Long toss c. Ground ball sequence drill d. 3-man relay e. Ground balls (Outfield – infield rotate players) f. Fly ball drill g. No look drills h. Quick toss	Time these drills and make a game of it.
4.	30 Mins	Assnt.	Split into 3 groups: a. HITTERS: Hitting (1 batter hitting, 1 batter on tee, 1 batter swing drills) b. FLY BALLS: Outfield, throw to bucket. c. GROUND BALLS: GB's, throw to bucket, rotate	Keep players moving. Can do all three at once. One coach for each group. Use buckets to limit the amount of time wasted chasing balls.
5.	20 Mins.	Assnt.	GAME LIKE SITUATION (Rotate) Include: a. Running b. Hitting c. Fielding d. Throwing	Make sure every player gets a look at every position. Review with players what they are doing w/ each batter.
6.	5 Mins.	H/C	Review	

Coaching Notes:
  a. From this point on you will need to address a new topic every day (see Master Schedule). Don't forget to use a stopwatch and whistle.

NOTES:

11.   PRACTICE SCHEDULE (Blank)

BABSON TIGERS
BASEBALL

Today's Emphasis: _____ Date: _____

Item	Time	Coach	Item	Comment

NOTES:

| |
| |
| |
| |
| |

12. *LAST THOUGHT ON PLANNING*

I met Mick Williams at a coaches' clinic I attended some time ago. He talked about the need for sound planning in order to run an effective baseball program. His article *Baseball is Only as Good as Your Planning* is worth reading.

Baseball is only as good as your planning

By: MICK WILLIAMS

Reprinted with the permission of the author.

Someone asked me what I see as the greatest coaching improvement opportunity in the average high school baseball program. The answer is simple, PLANNING!

Too many coaches rely on their personal knowledge of the game to carry them effectively through their team's practice. There are several problems I have with this. First, just because you know the game, it doesn't mean you know how to teach it. Second, good teaching requires considerable work and planning. A great ex-player who can't properly teach the game makes for a bad coach. A coach, who can teach the game but doesn't plan properly, also makes for a bad coach.

The greatest mistake a baseball coach can make is not properly preparing their season. Poor pre-season planning and bad practice schedules can be the greatest single most contributing factor to having a bad season. With all the training information available to today's coaching, I am amazed at the amount of coaches at the high school level that attempt to conduct practices with nothing prepared.

Baseball requires significant skill, speed and conditioning. A coach properly preparing for this is as important as the player's effort on the field. Using every second of every practice is crucial for a successful season. A good rule of thumb I use is planning time should be about half the field time. Two hours of practice should take about one hour of planning. Several things to keep in mind are:

- Every season should have a master plan.
- You should review the master plan with your players and coaches before your season begins. This insures they are aware of your expectations and goals
- The first practice sets the stage for the season. If your go in unprepared, don't expect much from your players. You set the example.
- Every practice should have a pre-established and posted schedule. The schedule should be broken down into three areas: warms ups and conditioning, skill development, and a game like component.
- Establish times for each activity and stick with them. Use a team manager with a stopwatch.
- Assistant coaches, team captains, and managers should have clearly established roles.
- Start practices on time and finish them on time. Players needing extra work are dealt with after the practice is over.
- Coaches are there to coach, not play. Make sure coaches and assistant coaches focus on their jobs and the players focus on theirs.

Conducting a practice that is ill prepared is unfair to the players and the game. Good planning makes a difference. When someone asks me, "What do you see as the greatest improvement opportunity on the average high school baseball program," the answer is simple - PLANNING!

How To Get And Keep The Players' Attention

Controlling your players and maintaining good discipline is key to a successful season. Without control, practice and game efficiency and effectiveness decline. One key element in maintaining control throughout the season is establishing rules and guidelines, and reviewing them with both the players and their parents at the start of the season. This insures there are no misinterpretations or surprises during the season and the players know exactly what is expected. The letters listed in Section 3 can be a great start.

While letters home will solve a majority of your potential problems, it won't solve them all. It is unreasonable to expect your players to behave themselves throughout the entire season. They're only kids. How you respond to these inevitable moments is as important as teaching the players how to throw a ball properly. Coaches over the years have asked me, "How do you discipline young players?" I have always felt uncomfortable with this question, especially when dealing with young children. I prefer to address this question by placing my efforts on establishing a good athletic learning environment at the beginning of the season, versus correcting a wayward process with draconian methods during the season. This is not to say we will not have our behavior challenges as coaches, we will. But I have found it more productive to look at this challenge from a, *positive action and behavior will result in rewards*, perspective.

1. *MOTIVATION THROUGH MOVEMENT*

Many coaches use running as punishment for bad behavior. In lieu of running I have found it more useful to use the time focusing on other key physical elements of the game. I call this *Motivation Through Movement (MTM)*. Most children know how to run so why waste precious practice time doing something they already know how to do? Activities such as the following can be more effective in training the players:

      a. Base running
      b. Stealing drills
      c. Drop step drills
      d. Dynamic stretching
      e. Ground ball chase drills
      f. Sliding drills
      g. Etc.

Many of the problems you will encounter with young players will be the players' inability to focus. We must remember they are children. They inherently have difficulties focusing. I learned long ago it is more effective adjusting to the players' inability to stay focused versus fighting it. Using MTM activities serve two purposes; first the players are learning something about the game, and second they become somewhat tired making it easier for them to focus on instruction.

2. *GUIDELINES FOR MTM*

When trying to get and keep the players attention, there are several guidelines that I use. They include:

a. Insure the consequences fit the transgression.
b. Be consistent in applying MTM. A small lapse of attention should result in a small MTM activity.
c. Insure the consequences are age and league appropriate. "Play to win," leagues such as traveling teams, AAU teams, or all-star teams will have greater consequences than those leagues established strictly for fun.
d. Keep what you are doing in perspective, they're children playing ball, not U.S. Army basic training recruits.
e. Nip your problems in the bud. They will not go away if you ignore them.
f. Never yell at the players (It's Ok to yell to them). Stay calm and in control.
g. Never embarrass a player in front of others.
h. Never reprimand a player for not understanding instruction. Responsibility for player instructional understanding lies with the coach.
i. Be careful about reprimanding a player for a fielding or hitting error. I have yet to see a player make an error on purpose.
j. Always follow up with an explanation as to what the player did wrong and what he/she needs to do to correct the problem.
k. Always end your motivation meetings and discussions on a positive note. Telling a player, "Hey Johnny, everyone makes mistakes. It's what you make of your mistakes that matters," is much more effective than, "You're a real pain Johnny! I've never seen a kid more disruptive than you! Shape up or ship out!"

To help you with what may be considered age appropriate for young players (Twelve and under). I use the following guidelines:

Table 6.3: Consequence Guidelines

Item	Consequence	Comments
Players not paying attention	MTM activity for the whole team	This instills some team pressure on those that have difficulty focusing. If more than one player is talking chances are that a good part of the team is not paying attention to what you are teaching.

Item	Consequence	Comments
One player not paying attention	MTM activity for the whole team	Again some peer pressure may be helpful. I would not however, use this more than a few times. If the problem persists take a team break and explain to the player that his/her inability to focus will result in them having to sit on the bench away from the team so as to not disrupt practice and waste precious time. After practice review this with the player explaining why his/her actions are disruptive. Offer helpful hints that may help keep them focused. Something as simple as, "Count to three before you talk," can sometimes be very helpful.
Players missing practice without a good excuse (i.e. medical, school, appointment, etc.)	Does not start game.	Many leagues require that every player participate in every game. Make it known however, that good performance during practice is rewarded with time on the field during a game. Those missing practice will not have as much play time as those that attend and work hard. If the problem persists, schedule a meeting with the parents.
Arguing with the coach.	Player sits	If you treat the players with respect, you should expect the same from them. When a player argues with coach I sit the player immediately and address the problem after practice. If the problem is serious I schedule a meeting with the parents. Further violations may result in suspension. Little League has guidelines for parents and coaches on how to handle serious issues.
Player fighting with one another.	Player sits	I sit the player immediately. I discuss the incident with the players involved and try to gain understanding of the problem. I would then give them the condition in which they need to return the next day. I have the players shake hands before going home. I follow up with both players before the start of the next practice or game to insure there are no remaining problems. Note – there is a difference between a disagreement and fight.

Arguing with umpires	Player sits	I sit the player immediately. I inform the players that any and all issues with the umpires are to be addressed by me, the coach, not them (Or their parents). I have them shake hands and apologize to the umpire before going home. I follow up with the player before the start of the next practice or game to insure there are no remaining problems. Note – there is a difference between a disagreement and an argument.
Late for practice	Extracurricular team activity	I use items such as cleaning the dug outs, policing up the paper on the field, etc. I don't make this a big deal of this if it's only one time. It's the parents that usually cause this problem. If the problem persists speak with the parents reminding them that it is unfair to the rest of the team, the coach, and their child as it wastes valuable practice time. Remember: "Start on time, finish on time."
Violation of safety rules	Stop play immediately and correct the problem	Review with the player immediately. If the problem is intentional and dangerous, remove the player from the game or practice. Review with the player and his or her parents after the practice or game.
Lack of effort	Lack of play time	I do not reward lack of effort with playtime, regardless of the player's talent. I would rather play a player with mediocre talent that works hard, than a great player who exhibits little interest in doing the job well. I take the player aside at the end of the game or practice and explain why they sat and what is expected for them to correct.

3. ASKING FOR HELP

As a coach, we must be aware that disruptive behavior can sometimes be a cry for help. Children sometimes exhibit bad behavior because of poor self-image, a feeling of inadequacy, problems at home, problem with peers, problems in school, or just normal issues with growing up. We do not need to be trained, certified youth counselors to help. Lending an ear and giving extra support and attention to those that need it, is sometimes all that is required. If you have a player however, that may have a more serious problem, seek the advise of your league officials.

4. TOKEN PLAYTIME

The following is an article I wrote some time ago concerning token playtime. It speaks for itself.

Token Play Time

A Player's Worst Moment, A Coach's Worst Excuse

By: Jake Patterson

Youth coaches, both experienced and inexperienced, sometimes defend and justify their starting and playtime decisions by using token playtime. Token playtime is the process of playing a bench player when there is no hope of winning the game, there is no way to lose it, or potential damage can be easily mitigated. It typically occurs in the last moments of a game. The coach scans the bench and without warning yells, "Jones, get in there and hit!" The startled player grabs a helmet and bat and runs to the plate unprepared for the next few seconds of his life.

More times than not, the nervous player performs poorly. In many cases the coach uses this to reinforce his or her decision not to play the player often or start the player. When the player inevitably fails, I have witnessed coaches turning to parents, other coaches, players or the fans and give them a, "See that's why I don't play him," look. The end result of the whole process is the player learns nothing and the coach misses the opportunity to build and teach both the player and the team.

Two things usually happen from a player's perspective. First, the player feels embarrassed and angry because he was unprepared for his only moment in the sun and was not given a fair opportunity to succeed.

The second thing that happens is the player and his parents see token playtime for what it is; an after thought for the untalented. Whether this is true or not from the coach's perspective is irrelevant in the eyes of the player and parents. They typically go home feeling bad about the game and their opportunity to contribute.

We all know stories of young players wanting to quit a team because they were not playing. I can remember my youngest son wanting to quit his middle school basketball team because the only time the coach would play him was when the team was winning by a lot or losing by a lot. The coach even had her token playtime players sit at the far end of the bench so they wouldn't interfere with the "real" basketball players. It resulted in destroying his love for the game. He wasn't the best, the tallest, or the most talented player, but he worked hard and was reliable, important athletic traits some coaches fail to recognize in their players. His coach looked at basketball as a five man game supported by random substitutes. This left the bench feeling isolated and the starters feeling overwhelmed. Few lessons were learned and no one had fun.

WHAT IS THE REASON FOR TOKEN PLAYTIME?

The reason for token playtime is simple: The coach wants to win! They play their best players in hopes of winning every game. While winning in itself is not a bad thing, it must be balanced with teaching and developing. Determining how much emphasis is placed on each is determined by the age of the players and the league in which you play.

67

The age of the players.

The younger the player, the more emphasis there is on development and teaching. Emphasis on winning must be age appropriate. Stump Merrill, a great Major League Baseball coach, helped me with this concept several years ago during a coaches' clinic. After listening to Stump talk about youth athletics, several of us developed a matrix that shows appropriate levels of teaching, developing, winning, fun, work the athletes must dedicate to the sport and time needed to play and practice, based on the type of league and age of the player. The results were eye opening. Each athletic level had varying amounts of emphasis in every category. The point is, that every level requires different coaching techniques and winning emphasis.

The type of league you play in.

A Minor League team will have different goals and objectives than a traveling AAU team that requires regional tryouts. The town team will lean more toward fun while the AAU team will lean more toward winning. While the commitment in time, money, and expectations are greater for the AAU team, both coaches must be aware of the development and teaching aspect of their responsibility.

WHO ARE THE TOKEN TIME PLAYERS?

Players who are usually subjected to token time are your least talented players. We all have coached players who struggle with basic skills no matter how hard they try. The important thing to remember as a coach is the reason they struggle can be either genetic or developmental. Some young players have the physical ability and attributes to play well, but they require time to develop. Others will never be good athletes, but should be afforded the same opportunities to contribute to the team. Other reasons for token playtime include:

Inexperienced coaches.

Few youth coaches come to coaching with any background or training in coaching. They are learning and simply miss things. They get wrapped up in the moment and forget about the player at the end of the bench.

Poor coaching.

Some coaches are just bad coaches. They want to win and care little about the player sitting the bench.

Favoritism.

Unfortunately, some coaches have players they like more than the other players. They overplay the favored players at the expense of the less favored players. This is difficult to hide and is usually detrimental to the team as well as the players involved.

Players who deserve little time.

Playtime is earned during practices. There are those that deserve little playtime because of poor practice habits. Establishing rules at the beginning of the season and reviewing them with players and parents help prevent misunderstandings here. Poor conduct in practice deserves less playtime in a game.

HOW TO PREVENT TOKEN PLAYTIME.

Next to cutting players at tryouts, deciding who plays is the most difficult decision a coach can make. There are several items a coach can do to help with this.

Come to games prepared.

Take a few minutes to establish a game plan. Going to a game prepared can eliminate oversights made during a game.

Recognize your job is to teach and develop.

Many youth coaches live their own athletic dreams through their players. They lose sight that the game is about the athlete. An old coach once told me, "Stop worrying about winning, you can't control it. The only thing you can control is how well you prepare your team and how well you prepare yourself."

Accept that a team is only a team when all members feel they are part of the team.

Every player should have a role. Examples include back-up infielder, reliever and pinch runner. To be successful everyone needs to know where he or she fits. Make the game about the kids, all the kids. Yes it is more fun to win, but you must balance that with a sense of fairness to all players.

Balance short-term goals with the long-term development of the team.

Win/loss records are important, but so is teaching and developing. A coach should be looking for every opportunity to play the younger players. This should be viewed as an investment in the team's future. Every game, every practice should be viewed as a teaching and development opportunity.

When presented the opportunity, try something VERY different.

When losing big or winning big try new things. It's fun and it gives you an opportunity to teach and to discover new talents. I had a young man struggled the entire season. He worked hard but just never seemed to catch on to what we were trying to teach. During a hopeless game I told all the players on the bench, "Ok, everyone's in! Where do you want to play?" Bob said he would like to try pitching. Good pitchers in our league, (High school) throw a fastball 70-80 MPH. Some hit the mid to high 80's. I felt there was no way he would survive one batter. It turns out that Bob's hero is the famous under-hand Korean pitcher Byung-Hyun Kim, a former starting pitcher for the Boston Red Sox. Bob went to the mound, threw his first pitch, knuckles almost dragging the ground ala Byung-Hyun Kim and hit the center of the strike zone with an 80-MPH fastball. When he completed his warm ups we were flabbergasted. How could we have possibly missed this! Bob didn't save the game that day, but I did find a potential pitcher. The point is there may be a diamond in the rough.

Providing the athletes a fair opportunity to succeed rather than an opportunity to fail is your most important job as a coach. Don't look to justify your playing and starting decisions with a few moments of unexpected time for your bench players. Keep everyone involved and develop roles for all players. Remember the game is for the players. *The future athletic memories of our children are being made today. Go and make good memories!*

Section 7. Basic Baseball/Softball Techniques

Throwing a Baseball

Throwing the ball properly is not an easy skill to teach or master, and is one of the most difficult skills to correct later when taught wrong. Several basic items to consider when teaching players to throw are as follows:

1. CHILDREN AND HOW THEY GROW AND THROW

Throwing a baseball properly is not a natural thing for the human body to do. Our muscles and bones are not made to comfortably throw a ball and we have to train our bodies to do it the most effective way. This takes a lot of time and proper instruction. The following is what you may see as the child develops:

Table 7.1: How a Child Throws

Age	League	Typical Throwing Technique
2-5	Pre Tee-Ball	Under hand throw, most times two-handed
5-8	Tee-Ball – Minor League	Throw starts in front of the body with arm traveling straight down the side of the body. Crossing the body is difficult.
8-10	Minor League – Little League	Modified baseball throw. Hand starts out back and is able to cross the body. Limited hip rotation.
11-12	Little League and older	Good baseball throwing technique. Hand across the body with good hip rotation.

The point here is to be patient. It is important you take all the time necessary to teach the players proper throwing technique, and remember; proper technique is taught one small step at a time.

2. *THE GRIP*
    a. Have players move to a two-finger grip as soon as they can, one finger width apart.
    b. The pads of the fingers should be across a seam with finger pressure applied slightly above the top knuckle. The best grip is a four-seam grip (Shown below). The player should see a "C" off the side of the fingers.

Four Seam Grip

    c. Place the thumb under the ball directly below the fingers, with the bony part of the thumb on the ball.
    d. Palm of the hand should not touch the ball. There should be a visible gap between the fingers and thumb.
    e. When starting the throw from behind the head, ensure the players keep their throwing fingers on top of the ball.

3. *THE THROW*
    a. Start the throw with the glove and ball in front of the chest. Separate the hands such that the arms are extended on plane with the target.
    b. When ready to throw, the throwing hand should be even with the top of the head and behind the body, fingers on top. The body should be in a "bow and arrow stance," with the back of the glove pointing toward the target, throwing hand directly back.
    c. Upper part of the throwing arm should be somewhat parallel to the ground.

74

d. Throw the ball off the fingertips with backspin. This allows the ball to carry more.

e. Have the players throw at a target. Pick a spot on the receiver's chest. Avoid using the entire chest as a target and have them pick a six-inch circle in the middle of the chest. Big target, big margin of error. Small target, small margin of error.

f. Step toward the target with front foot.

g. Throw across the body at a 45-degree angle, finishing with the throwing hand in the opposite "pocket."

h. Rotate hips finishing by planting the toe of the throwing foot in the ground out in front of the throwing side of the body.

i. Recover immediately, expecting the returned throw.

Who Quits Baseball?

At a recent baseball and softball clinic I met Harvey Dorfman. Harvey is a well-known sports psychologist and has been around baseball for many decades. He asked our group, "At what level do you think most kids quit playing baseball?" We were surprised when he said Little League. Watch the pressures you place on your child and players. Make sure the game stays fun. By the way I would highly recommend Harvey's book Coaching The Mental Game.

Catching a Baseball

Catching a baseball is a basic skill of the game. Again, it's more difficult to correct bad habits than it is to teach the proper techniques. Catching the ball properly should always include both hands when coaching Little League. Too many young players see the one-handed catches made by the pros and feel this is the way to catch a ball. At a young age it is not! Do not let them do it! Other items include:

1. THE GLOVE

    a. Little Leaguers should have a properly fitted leather glove. Avoid cheap plastic gloves. They fall apart quickly and affect the player's ability to learn.

    b. Gloves come in different sizes and types. There are softball and baseball gloves, catcher's mitts, first baseman's mitts, infield gloves and outfield gloves. All are different and, all come in different sizes. A 10" - 11" infielder mitt is a good place to start for most Little Leaguers. Maximum size for Little League is twelve inch. The size of the glove is usually printed in the inside palm area and is measured from the top of the forefinger to the base of the palm. The following chart can be used as a guideline:

Table 7.2: Glove Sizes

Age (Years)	League	Position	Glove Size
5-6	Tee-Ball	All	10" – 10 ½"
7-8	Minor League	All	10 ½" – 11"
9-12 Little League	Little League Middle School	All	11" – 11 ½"
12+ Little	Middle School Junior League Senior League High School	Outfield	12" – 12 ½"
12+	Middle School Junior League Senior League High School	Infield	11" 11 ½"
12+	Middle School Junior League Senior League High School	First base	12" – 12 ½"

   c. The players should break in their glove by first oiling it with a good brand glove oil and by working the glove. Working the glove is accomplished by bending the top of each finger and thumb to the inside palm of the glove repeatedly. This emulates the way our hands work. Avoid folding the glove through the web.

   d. Using a batter's glove on the glove hand will help increase the life of the glove by preventing dirt and sweat from breaking down the leather.

   e. The difference between a mitt and a glove is a glove has fingers and a mitt does not. The first baseman and the catcher are the only players permitted to use a mitt on the field.

2. THE BASE (Lower Body)

Catching the ball starts with a good base. Get your players used to a good athletic position. They should be in this position every time they are expecting the ball. I have the players develop a routine before each pitch or catch that allows them to get into a good defensive position.

   a. Feet apart, slightly more than shoulder width apart.

   b. Back straight.

   c. Knees slightly bent.

   d. Weight remains on the balls of the feet. You should be able to slide a piece of paper under their heels.

e.   Stay balanced.
f.   Keep feet moving and stay loose.

3.   *THE UPPER BODY*
a.   Head up with both eyes looking for the ball.
b.   Hands out front with fingers spread up and out.
c.   Palms to the ball. When in the field do not allow players to get into the habit of resting their hands on their knees when in the ready position.

4.   *THE CATCH*
a.   Always have the player move to the ball versus waiting for the ball to come to them.
b.   Catch the ball out in front of the body.
c.   Transfer the ball fluidly. Use "butterfly" technique to transfer the ball.
d.   Above the waist, fingers should point up and make "W's".
e.   Below the waist, fingers should point down and make "M's".
f.   Avoid one-handed catches. One-handed catches are prone to more errors and it is more difficult to transition the ball to the throw.

5.   *GROUND BALLS*
a.   Start with a good athletic position.
b.   Hands out front with the palms to the ball.
c.   Stay relaxed and keep the feet moving.
d.   Catch the ball slightly glove side, thigh to belly.
e.   When catching a ground ball, keep the glove at a 45-degree angle to the ground. You want to the palm of the glove facing the ball, not the fingers.
f.   Use a clamshell catch. Glove underneath, throwing hand on top, ready to capture the ball.
g.   Watch the ball go into the glove; some coaches describe this as, "button to button" (Button on the top of the hat moves toward the belly button).
h.   Transfer the ball fluidly. Use "butterfly" technique to transfer the ball.
i.   Teach the players to move to the ball versus letting the ball come to them.

"Baseball is the only field of endeavor where a man can succeed three times out of ten and be considered a good performer."

- Ted Williams

Table 7.3: Short Toss Relay

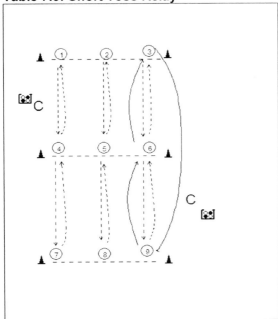

SHORT TOSS RELAY DRILL

1. Sequence for this drill should be short toss, long toss, quick toss, and then short toss relay.
2. Insure players are properly stretched before throwing. Remember, "Warm up to throw, don't, throw to warm up."
3. Key for coaches is to watch for technique and insure players turn glove side.
4. Match players by arm strength.
5. Have players throw to a six-inch circle in the center of the chest as a target.

Table 7.4: Double Play Drill

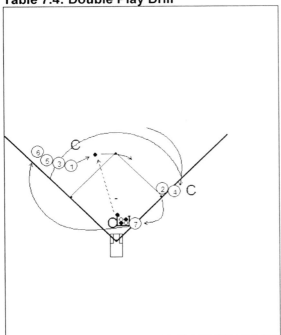

DOUBLE PLAY DRILL

1. On "Go!" coach tosses ball underhand out in front of player breaking to second base.
2. Player tags second base and throws to first.
3. Player rotates from shortstop to first to the bucket.
4. Coach at shortstop is teaching how to receive the ball out front and how to tag second base and make throw to first or how to throw or flip the ball to second base.
5. Coach at first base is teaching how to catch the ball, how to move to the bag, and how to find and touch the bag with their throwing foot.
6. Move to coach-tossed ground balls.

Table 7.5: Ground Ball Circle Drill

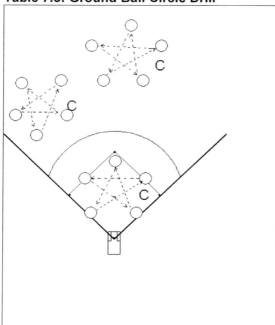

GROUND BALL CIRCLE DRILL

1. Divide players in groups of five (more is OK).
2. Start with small circles, no gloves.
3. Balls are received and redirected to next player using both hands out front.
4. Have players step back and use gloves.
5. Teach a good ready-set position, i.e. feet apart, back straight, player on ball of the feet, knees bent, head up, hands out front.
6. Go to two balls as the players improve.

Catching and Throwing Drills

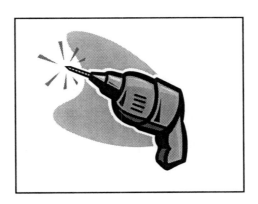

There are literally hundreds of effective age-appropriate throwing and catching drills. If you have a problem with catching or throwing there is a drill to fix it. A little research can make a big difference. If you are having difficulty finding the right drill contact us at pattersonsports@yahoo.com. The following are several basic drills appropriate for the youth levels:

a. *TENNIS BALL DRILL*: Tennis balls are great training aids for young children. It is difficult to catch a tennis ball with one hand, forcing the players to use both hands. This teaches the players to involve the throwing hand early. Best of all tennis balls don't hurt. This helps build player confidence. You can also use injury reduced balls, tee balls, or Incredaballs. They are similar to baseball but softer.

b. *ONE HANDED SELF-TOSS*: Toss the ball in the air with the throwing hand and catch it with the throwing hand. Have the players get used to rotating the ball finding a four-seam grip. This drill gets the players used to moving the ball quickly in their hands to find the seams.

c. BACK OF THE GLOVE DRILL: Use the back of the glove to catch the ball. This teaches two-hand involvement with the catching process. The players can't catch a ball with the back of the glove unless the throwing hand captures the ball.

d. *SHORT TOSS – LONG TOSS*: Have the players start about twenty feet apart. After 15-20 throws move the players back several feet. Repeat the process until they reach their maximum throwing distance. Match the players by their arm strength, size, and the distance they can throw. Don't put your best player with your worst. You know the players have reached their maximum distance for this drill when they need a small skip step to throw the ball hard enough to reach the target. It is not the intent of this drill to see how far the players can throw. It's used to loosen and strengthen their arms and legs.

e. *QUICK TOSS*: Used only after the players have warmed up. Match the players based on ability. The intent of this drill is to transition the ball quickly not throw the ball hard. This drill is good for hand-eye coordination and teaching how to move the feet. Great drill to time and count. Use 30-second cycles. Remember to catch the ball out front. "Butterfly" transition, move the feet, throw, finish and recover. Use care with this drill, as you do not want to have players hurt their arms.

f. *"SET, READY" DRILL*: On "SET" the player prepares for the infield ready position. On "READY" infielder sets hands down and in front, fingers out, knees bent, eyes on the ball, head up, back straight. This helps establish a defensive routine for every pitch. While every player will be comfortable with something different I start with, throwing foot forward one step, glove foot up and then a slight shuffle side to side.

g. *ONE STEP CROSS OVER DRILL*: Players start in the set position. Coach blows whistle and points right or left. The player uses a cross over step and establishes a good ground ball catching stance. Coaches check for movement and recover techniques. To finish the drill roll a ball to the player once he or she reaches his or her position.

h. *3-STEP CROSS OVER DRILL*: Same as above except player moves three steps.

i. *2-LINE REACTION DRILL*: Same as above, except players are formed into two lines about 30-60 feet apart facing each other. Coach sets up behind the line catching the ball. Coach points right or left. On "Go!" the opposite player rolls the ball in the direction the coach points, about five feet to the side of the fielder. Rotate players after several tries. Teaches players how to move laterally.

j. *SHORT HOP DRILL*: In this drill have the players set up about ten feet apart. Have them bounce the ball about three feet from their partner. As they improve, have the players bounce the ball closer to each other. Do both forehand and backhand. You can start this drill as a line drill using several coaches.

k. *POP FLY, NO LOOK DRILL*: Player 1 starts on one knee looking down. Player 2 throws the ball in the air and says, "Go!" when the ball is at its peak. Player 1 stands, locates the ball and makes the catch out in front. Rotate every three catches.

l. *AWAY AND FIND DRILL*: Player gives ball to coach and runs away from coach. On "Now!" coach throws ball to player. Player quickly turns, locates the ball and catches out in front. This can be added to by having the player set and throw to a bag. This is similar to a football buttonhook drill.

m. *COACH GIVE DRILL:* In this drill the player gets extended as if throwing, glove to target, throwing hand extended back fingers on top. When good form is established, the coach sticks a ball into throwing hand and player completes throwing cycle. This a great drill to teach proper throwing form and technique.

Table 7.6: Two Coach Ground Ball Rotation Drill

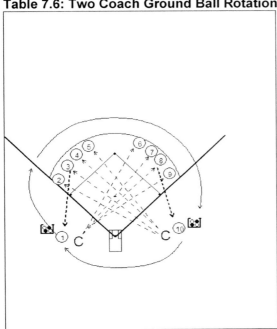

TWO COACH GROUND BALL ROTATION DRILL

1. Coach hits ground balls across the infield in rotation.
2. Ball is caught and then thrown to the same side as the player's position opposite of the coach hitting.
3. Everyone gets one ground ball and then rotates one position.
4. Players rotate into the buckets to catch for the coaches.
5. Teach the players to keep a ball in the coach's hand. This makes the drill more efficient.
6. Have players shag their own missed balls and throw them in as not to interrupt the rotation.

Table 7.7: Outfield Ground Ball/Fly Ball Drill

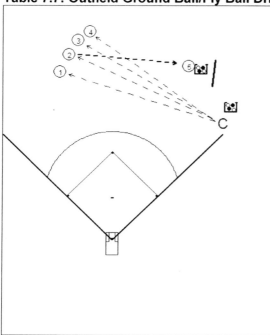

OUTFIELD GROUND BALL/FLY BALL DRILL

1. Great drill to run during any infield ground ball drill.
2. Coach sets up in the outfield away from the infield.
3. Use a pitching machine if available. Most pitching machines are capable of throwing fly balls a great distance accurately. 4. Balls are thrown to a target set up in the outfield.
5. Player manning the bag yells, "Hit me, hit me!" and gives a big target with extended hands. You can also practice hitting the bag to simulate throwing a runner out. Use a screen behind the bag so you do not waste time chasing balls.
6. Bucket is brought in to the coach on the rotation.
7. Vary the type of balls hit, i.e. short fly balls, long fly balls, high fly balls, shallow fly balls, and ground balls. When doing so however, do so in groups in order to keep the practice efficient.

Table 7.8: Zig Zag Drill

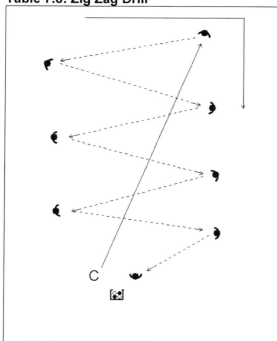

ZIG ZAG DRILL

1. Coach hits ball to the far corner.
2. Ball is zig-zagged across the field.
3. Players rotate clock-wise after a specific amount of ground balls.
4. One player rotates to the coach and flips balls to the coach.
5. All errors are disregarded and policed up after a cycle is complete.
6. Make a game of it by seeing how many balls you can keep going at one time.
7. Good indoor drill (Use Incredaballs).

Table 7.9: Roll And Go's

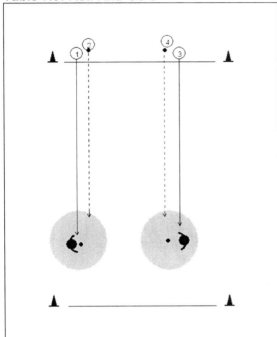

ROLL AND GO'S

1. 1 & 3 are the fielders (1 is right handed, 3 is left-handed).
2. On a whistle 2 and 4 roll the ball to a specific area (dark area).
3. 1 and 3 chase the ball down sets over the top of the ball, bare hands the ball with throwing side away from the throwing target.
4. Players 1 and 3 sets to throws and throws ball to 2 and 4.
5. 1 sets with right side back (right handed), 3 sets left side back (left handed).
6. Players return and alternate with partners.

"I'd like to be remembered. I'd like to think that someday two guys will be talking in a bar and one of them will say something like, 'Yeah, he's a good shortstop, but he's not as good as ole Ripken was.' "

- Cal Ripken

The Basics of Hitting

Many young hitters today try to emulate the homerun hitters of Major League Baseball. Although very talented, they do little to help the Little Leaguer. Many professional batting instructors and coaches would rather use the styles of Ted Williams and Joe Dimagio as examples. Many regard them as two of the purest hitters the game ever saw. Who the young players emulate is not as important as making sure they start with the basics. Having heroes and role models are important for every child, but it's the coach's job is to make sure they pick the right ones. Using one of today's many long ball hitters that seldom leg out a ground ball would not be a good example.

Hitting can be broken down into several basic elements. Some of the following items may have to be slightly adjusted, as they may be too complicated for the real young players. You will need to get a feel for what your players are capable of when you begin teaching. Stick to the basics and work up. A good swing has a lot to do with muscle memory. Teach it right and their muscles will take over.

1. *THE BAT*
    a. The Little League metal bat is usually 27"–32" long and can weigh 3-9 ounces less than its length. Many leagues have restrictions on the length to weight ratio. As an example a bat that is thirty inches long and twenty-five ounces in weight is a minus five bat (25 – 30 = -5).
    b. You should familiarize yourself with your league requirements. Baseball has established the BESR (Bat Exit Speed Ratio) standard to regulate and standardize baseball bats. Bats that meet BESR requirements are marked on the barrel of the bat.

c. Older youth leagues, such as middle school, Junior League, Senior League, and American Legion Ball use a minus three (-3) bat. A –3 bat best emulates a typical northern ash wooden bat controlling the effectiveness a wide length to weight ratio can have. This limits the speed in which the ball comes off the bat.

d. To determine appropriate bat size for a young batter, have the batter hold the bat straight out, parallel to the ground, by its knob with the throwing hand. They should be able to hold the bat steady for fifteen seconds. If they waiver or it falls, the bat is too heavy. If they can hold it steady for more than twenty seconds then the bat may be too light.

e. The following is a good starting point for bat size selection.

Table 7.10: Bat Sizes (In Inches)

Batter's Weight/ Height	3'-3'6"	3'7"-4'0"	4'0"-4'6"	4'7" –5"	5'1"-5'6"	5'7"- 6'
Under 50 lbs	26	27	28	29		
50-60 lbs	27	28	29	30	30	
61-70	27	28	29	30	30	
71-80		28	29	30	31	32
81-90		28	29	30	31	32
91-100		29	30	30	31	32
101-110		29	30	31	32	32

f. Make sure the grips are in good order. They are inexpensive and are easy to repair.

g. Check for cracks. Yes, metal bats can and do crack. Look for tiny stress cracks. Once a bat cracks, destroy and discard it.

2. *THE HANDS (Grip)*

a. In order to get a good grip on the bat, Ted Williams once said, "Grab the bat like an axe." This may be the easiest way to teach young players. Have them make believe they are chopping wood on the plate with the bat. Bring the bat straight overhead and have them check their hands. They should be in a good relative position. When set, have them point their first fingers up. Both fingers should both point in the same direction.

b. Hold the bat with the bottom three fingers and the base of the thumbs.

c. Grip with the lower part of the fingers, not the fingertips.

d. Don't wrap the hand around the bat.

e. Hold bat lightly. The grip should get tighter as the batter swings the bat. I use a scale of one to ten (1 – 10) to best describe this to children. Three being loose enough for the bat to easily slide through the hands when tugged by another person. Ten being as tight as the batter can possibly hold it. The swing starts with a three and increases through the swing until the player makes contact with the ball. The grip being 10 at contact.

3. *THE STANCE*

    a. To determine proper distance from the plate, touch the top of the bat to the outside of the plate with the front hand. This will ensure the whole plate is covered.
    b. Have the players set up in the middle of the box. Do not place too much emphasis on whether the batter is up in the box or back in the box. The average Little League pitcher cannot throw hard enough to make a difference to the batter. The key is to cover the strike zone.
    c. Feet should be slightly more than shoulder width apart.
    d. Slight bend at the knees, back straight.
    e. Weight on the balls of your feet.
    f. Load up on back foot. To check a proper load, use the bat as a pendulum by placing the knob of the bat at the player's belly button and let the bat hang loosely. Move the body back until the top part of the bat is hanging over the inside of the back foot.
    g. Keep the swing compact. Start the hands one-fist length from the body, even with the back of the back of the shoulder. Hands that are extended too far back or are extended too far from the body will make the swing awkward and ineffective.
    h. Bat is held at a 45-degree angle off shoulder. Arms should start in an inverted "V."
    i. An imaginary line off the length of the bat should touch slightly behind the far side of the plate.

4. *THE HEAD*

    a. Head stays straight up with eyes parallel to the ground. This is very important!
    b. Both eyes facing forward. In order to be effective, the batter needs to see the ball with both eyes in order to properly judge distance. Tell the batter to close their front eye and ask, "Does your nose block part of the pitcher?" If it does, the batter must turn his head more toward the pitcher.
    c. Keep the mouth slightly open. It relaxes the face and keeps the eyes opened.
    d. Head should stay as still as possible during the swing. Head movement of any kind makes it difficult to see the ball properly.

5. *THE UPPER BODY*

    a. Shoulders parallel to the ground. A good way to demonstrate this is to place a bat at each shoulder and see if the bat is parallel to the ground facing the pitcher.

    b. Stay tall. Don't slouch or bend over the plate.

    c. Chin up and locked at the front shoulder. There should be a two to three finger space between chin and shoulder.

    d. Head over the back knee.

6. *THE STRIDE*

    a. Keep hands and weight back as long as possible.

    b. Don't jump at the ball or lose balance. Don't fall forward.

    c. The stride is a slight step forward, with the front toe pointed slightly in, weight on the ball of the foot.

    d. Train the hitters to start their stride directly to the pitcher. A right-handed batter stepping toward third, or a left-handed batter stepping toward first, opens the hips and won't allow for a good swing.

7. *THE SWING*

    a. Get the players to think hit every pitch. It's a lot easier to stop a swing than it is to start one.

    b. Do not allow the players to lose their balance or move their head when they separate and begin their swing.

    c. Swing shoulder to shoulder. Chin starts at the front shoulder and finishes at the back shoulder.

    d. Palm up, palm down through the hitting zone. Back palm up, front palm down. Have the players practice this off to the side to get a good feel for this.

    e. Roll the wrists after the bat travels through the hitting zone. The bat is through the hitting zone typically after the back arm is fully extended. Too early and the batter will lose power at contact.

    f. Demonstrating good timing with a golf swing can be effective. It will give the players a feeling for how their timing should look.

    g. The sequence of the swing is, set, load, separate, swing.

> *"My motto was always to keep swinging. Whether I was in a slump or feeling badly or having trouble off the field, the only thing to do was keep swinging."*
>
>   - Hank Aaron

Hitting Advice

1. Teach the strike zone to the hitter. Get the player accustomed to a ball and a strike early. Having the batter at the plate while holding the ball in the all corners of the strike zone can help. A great training aid here is a hitting stick.
2. Always use your best throwing coach during batting practice. It must be someone who can throw strikes. Batters become frustrated quickly with someone who cannot throw well and begin to develop bad batting habits.
3. When using a pitching machine, present the ball to the batter before loading. It's important that you establish a routine that emulates the timing of the pitcher.
4. When throwing batting practice, throw a ball every 7-10 seconds depending on the batter. This allows the batter enough time to recover and reset properly. Set up the pitching machine before practice.
5. Batting practice is a good time to rotate the players through the different field positions. This gives everyone a feel for every position (See appendix).
6. Work with hitters having difficulty hitting off to the side. Don't stop the practice for one player.
7. Use a pitching screen when throwing batting practice; an injured coach really puts a damper on a practice. One year I spent a bunch of hours in an emergency room, compliments of a line drive hit by a twelve-year-old.
8. Have players in the outfield throw to a bucket at second base.
9. Have infielders throw to a bucket on first base.
10. Instead of having players throw each ball to the coach to get them in, have them run full buckets to the mound and dump them into the coach's bucket. This is much more efficient and allows for more hitting practice.
11. Batting practice can be boring. Have a coach off to the side hitting ground balls to the outfield and infield. Make sure you time it such that two balls are not going to the fielders at one time.
12. On deck batters should be timing their swings, especially during a game. A good guideline here is to have the players swing, timing their swings such that they hear the crack of the catcher's mitt just as they finish getting through the hitting zone.

"After I hit a home run I had a habit of running the bases with my head down. I figured the pitcher already felt bad enough without me showing him up rounding the bases."

-Mickey Mantle

Hitting Drills

a. *SHOULDER-TO-SHOULDER CHIN DRILL*: Same as above. Used for players having difficulty keeping their head up and still. Start with the chin at front shoulder; swing through with the chin ending at the back shoulder. Make sure the head stays as still as possible.

b. *SLAP THE MONKEY DRILL*:
    1. Have the hitter set up in the batter's box with his front hand on his stomach and the back hand straight up, palm open as if taking an oath.
    1. On "Set," player moves to a good neutral hitting position, head looking forward with both eyes to the pitcher. Batter stays lose with some movement.
    2. On "Load," player moves weight back to ready position.
    3. On "Separate," player moves the front foot toward the pitcher, foot turned slightly in. The back hand moves slightly back, keeping the palm of the hand facing first base for right-handers and third base for left-handers.
    2. On "Go," player starts swing with hip and imagines slapping a monkey in the head; belt high and slightly in front of front hip.
    3. Using a batting tee with a Nerf ball waist high, in front is a good way to conduct this drill.

c. *1-HANDED SMALL BAT DRILL*:
    1. Start with the front hand. Using soft toss, a coach flipping the ball to the hitter from a few feet from the side of the batter, have the batter swing, concentrating on the knob of the bat coming down in a straight diagonal line to the ball. The swing should resemble a diagonal cut down to the ball and push after contact. The idea here is form not hitting the ball hard.
    2. The back hand should be similar to the, "Slap the Monkey Drill." Knob of the bat cuts diagonally down, palm up through the hitting zone, wrist rolling after contact.
    3. A good check in completing both drills properly is to insure back foot is on its ball, some coaches call it squashing the bug, the heal is straight up with the bottom of the foot facing straight back.

d. *1-KNEE SWING DRILL* (Both hands): Same as above except on one knee, non-throwing knee down. This works the upper body.

e. *BATTING TEE*: The batting tee can be a very useful training device for children if used properly. Ensure hitters are using all the techniques discussed above. There are many books that feature batting tee drills and I encourage coaches to research them before using a batting tee.

1. Do not allow players to just go up and smack the ball. They must concentrate on proper technique.
2. Batter faces the imaginary pitcher, concentrating on set up while looking down field.
3. When the batter is ready, they take a deep breath, set, load, separate and swing, hitting the top inside part of the ball.
4. If hitting into a fence, use tennis balls, as hard balls will damage the fence.
5. Coaches can effectively watch two or three stations at a time.
6. Have one player load while another is hitting.

Table 7.11: Batting Cage Stations

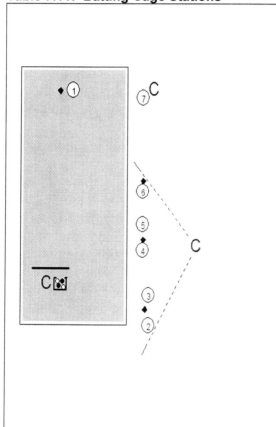

BATTING CAGE STATIONS

Running effective batting stations with a cage can be a complicate task, especially with young players. The following is a recommendation for the Little League level.

1. 1- Hitter.
2. 2- Soft toss hitter.
3. 3- Soft toss tosser.
4. Tee drill hitter.
5. Tee drill loader.
6. Bombat/ single hand drills, with or with out tee.
7. Coach 1 loading-pitching machine.
8. Coach 2 coaching tee drills.
9. Coach 3 coaching on deck and hitter.
10. On "Rotate!" players rotate to next position. Hitter and on deck player picks up balls in cage.
11. Keep number of hits to 10-15. More controlled rotations are better than a lot of hits in one session.
12. Coach at the pitching machine should present the ball to the hitter and establish a routine that would emulate the timing of a pitcher.
13. Use tennis balls when conducting soft toss and tee drills. Hit into the side of the cage.
14. Separating a long cage into two short cages with a screen or tarp allows you to have two cages going at the same time.

Table 7.12: Three Team Rotation

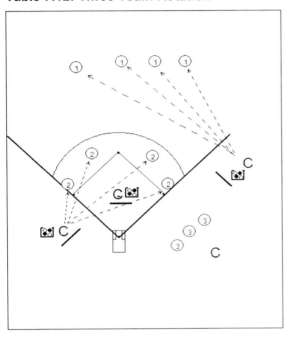

THREE TEAM ROTATION

1. Everyone hits 10-15 hits and then rotates. More swings will tire the batter limiting their ability to learn properly.
2. Coach 1 hits fly balls to team 1.
3. Coach 2 hits ground balls to team 2.
4. Coach 3 runs the on deck drills. Drills can include, tee drills, Bombats, one-handed drills, and soft toss.
5. Coach 4 throws hitting practice.
6. Use coaching screens for protection.

Note: The key here is to keep things moving. Batters that are having difficulties should be taken aside or helped after practice.

Table 7.13: 3-Box Stride Drill

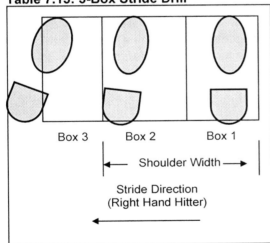

Box 3   Box 2   Box 1

← Shoulder Width →

Stride Direction
(Right Hand Hitter)

←

3-BOX STRIDE DRILL

1. Dark areas indicate the area of the foot where weight should be placed, the balls of the feet.
2. When starting the swing, 70% of the weight should be on the back foot.
3. When stepping to box three, ensure the hitters have the heel of the front foot turned slightly out toward the mound. This helps with proper swing rotation
4. Teach the young players to start their stride directly toward the pitcher. You can work on other variations of this later.
5. While striding forward the hands move back.
6. Great separation drill.

"People ask me what I do in winter when there's no baseball. I'll tell you what I do. I stare out the window and wait for spring."
- Roger Hornsby

Bunting

Bunting is an essential and important part of the offensive game. It is used to put pressure on the opponents and to move runners. Although bunting is not allowed at the lower levels of Little League, it should be taught properly at the levels that allow it. Here are several considerations when teaching batters how to bunt:

1. *TYPES OF BUNTING*

There are several types of bunts, which are used for different reasons. At the Little League level the most important bunt to teach is the sacrifice bunt. Different bunts include:

a. Sacrifice bunt: The sacrifice bunt is used to move the runners. There is little done by the batter to mask its intent. As its name suggests, you are sacrificing the batter for the sake of moving the runners.

b. Drag bunt: The batter is trying to catch the infield off guard. The move is quicker and the batter attempts to drag the ball up the base line as he breaks to first base. The intent is to catch the infield off guard

c. Squeeze bunt: The squeeze bunt is executed with less than two outs and is used to score the runner on third. This must be carefully executed by both batter and runner in order for the squeeze to work. The bunted ball needs to be hit to the weak side of the field and far enough from the plate to give the runner time to score. Remember the Little League runner can't leave the bag until the ball crosses the plate.

d. Slash bunt: The slash bunt is the most difficult bunt to teach and is usually only used at the older levels. The slash bunt is a feint at a normal bunt with the batter pulling the bat back at the last second and hitting an infield ground ball. It is used to draw the infield in and get a base hit.

2. *THE BUNT*

There are many techniques and nuances to bunting. There are books written on just this subject alone. In an attempt to keep things easy, I would suggest the following basic steps:

a. The batter stands as far in front of the batter's box as they can. This gives them the best opportunity to hit the ball in fair territory.

b. The move starts by rotating the hips so they finish somewhat perpendicular to the pitcher. This is accomplished by keeping the feet in place and rotating on the balls of the feet. Toes finish by pointing in the direction of the pitcher.

c. Knees are bent.

d. The bat is "presented" to the ball by sliding top hand up the barrel of the bat, keeping the fingers behind the bat at the same time the batter rotates.

e. At the Little League level, try to keep the bat as parallel to the ground as possible. This gives the best opportunity to make contact with the ball.

f. Keep the bat out and in front of the plate and in fair territory.

g. Target the top half of the ball.

h. The objective at contact is to absorb the energy of the ball versus hitting it.

3. *BUNTING DRILLS*

Again, as with every other skill there are a great number of bunting drills. The two that I would recommend for this level, other than live practice, are the back of the glove bunt and the bunt cone drill.

a. Back of the glove drill: A great drill at the Little League level is to pair off the players facing each other. Player 1 will be the batter; player 2 will be the pitcher. Have player 1 get in a batting stance. Player 2 tosses the ball under hand to player 1. Player 1 bunts the ball with the back of the glove. This allows the coach to train the whole team at once. Once player 1 gets the concept, rotate and repeat with player number 2.

b. Cone Drill: Set up two sets of cones, two on the first base side and two on the third base side about three feet from each other, perpendicular to the foul line and about ten feet up the foul line. Set the batters up into teams and let them compete against each other by bunting the ball between the cones. Scoring is:

Table 7.14: Bunt Drill Scoring

Points Awarded	Requirement
3 Points	Through the cones, good technique.
2 Points	Through the cones, Less than good technique.
1 Point	Missed the cones, good technique.
0 Points	Missed the cones and less than good technique.
-1 Points	Popped up the ball

Table 7.15: Bunt Cone Drill

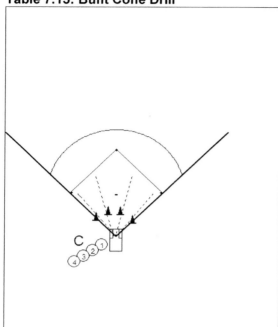

BUNT CONE DRILL

1. Form and proper methods is key. On deck coach is used to correct individual problems.
2. Ball must go through the set of cones. Coach states which cones they want to have the ball go through before the pitch.
3. Make a game of it.
4. Use bunt signals to test the player's knowledge of signals.

> *"There was a point at which I thought I'd never get the most valuable player, especially the years I played at Minnesota. We never won a pennant there, we were far away from the big media centers of Los Angeles and New York, and I wasn't a flashy power hitter but a guy who hit to spots, who <u>bunted</u> and stole bases."*
>
> - Rod Carew

Base Running

"If my uniform doesn't get dirty, I haven't done anything in the baseball game."

-Rickey Henderson

Base running is one of the most under-taught skills in baseball and softball, but can be the greatest offensive weapon on your team when executed properly. Aggressive base runners like Maury Wills, Lou Brock, and Rickey Henderson have all made their mark on the game because of their running skills and abilities. Every Little League coach should take the time to teach the proper mechanics of running.

1. *KEY ITEMS FOR THE RUNNER*
   a. The runner must always know the situation. Teach them to ask themselves "What do I do if the ball is hit?" Every pitch.
   b. The runner's job is to start the movement toward the next base; the coach's job is to stop it.
   c. When on base, the runner should anticipate every pitch in the dirt.
   d. Teach the players to, make a decision and live with it.
   e. The runner should always be aware of the location of the ball.
   f. Once the decision is made to steal, the runner's primary focus is the next base.

2. *LEADS*
   There are two parts of a proper lead, the primary lead and the secondary lead. Both are needed for good base running. Although we do not technically use a primary lead at the Little League level, the players should be aware and understand that there are two components to a good lead.

3. *PRIMARY LEAD*
   Move to the primary position off first base by:
   a. Right foot steps toward the mound one full step.
   b. Left foot crosses behind the right foot.
   c. Right foot shuffles out right, followed by a left foot shuffle.
   d. Stay low, hands out front and anticipate the dive back to the bag.

e. Never go beyond the point of no return. This point is different for every runner. Have the players find their own point of no return at practice.

f. Always be aware of where the infielders are. A good habit for the runners to develop is to physically point at the infielders.

g. Have the runner get the signal from the third base bag.

h. If a coach wants to give new instructions, have the runner return to the bag before giving the new signal.

i. When talking to a runner at first or third make sure the runner watches the ball while listening to you.

j. Always have the players acknowledge they understand the signal by touching their helmets. If they don't, call time out and talk to them. After a few times, they'll get it.

k. A primary lead off second base is several normal steps off the bag while facing the pitcher.

l. A primary lead off third base is a shuffle step in foul territory facing the pitcher.

4. *SECONDARY LEAD*

a. The best technique to teach runners is, out far, back fast. Avoid dancing. It serves little purpose and slows the game down. Doing it once in a while to rattle the defense is fine. Showboating detracts from the game and the runner loses focus on what they are supposed to be doing.

b. When on third base, runners go down foul, and return fair. Going down foul ensures that a runner hit by the ball is not called out. Returning fair hides the bag from the catcher.

5. *FACING THE FLY BALL AND TAGGING*

a. When tagging, always face the ball. Back foot on the bag, runner goes when ball is caught.

b. The distance in which the runner moves to the next base during a fly ball to the outfield varies depending upon the situation, speed of the runners, the ability of the fielders, how deep the ball is hit, and the maturity level of the runner. The following chart is a good place to begin when teaching how far down the baseline a Little League runner should move on a fly ball to the outfield. Bear in mind these are guidelines.

Table 7.16: Tagging on a Fly Ball You Expect to be Caught

Runner On	Location of the Outfield Fly Ball	Runner
First Base	Right Field Center Field	Half way down facing the fly ball.
First Base	Left Field	Two-thirds down, facing left field.
Second Base	Right Field Center Field Left Field	One-third the way down, facing the ball.
Third Base	All Fields	Automatically tag and go on coach's signal.

6. *DIVING BACK TO THE BAG*

    a. During a close pick-off attempt, have the players dive back to the bag low with their face away from the ball, reaching for the bag with the right hand. This presents the back of the helmet to the ball and tag, preventing injury to the face and head.

7. *SLIDING*

    a. The easiest way to teach how to slide is to begin with a static figure four. The steps include:

        1. Start with the players lying on the ground on their backs.

        2. Move one leg up under the top leg placing the ankle under the knee of the top leg, toes pointed up.

        3. Top leg stays extended and slightly bent at the knee.

        4. Upper body sits up with hands up and out with palms facing the base they are sliding toward.

    b. Once the players understand how they should look when they are sliding have them move into a crab stance and on "Go!" have them pop to the figure four. This helps them understand how to move their body to the figure four position.

    c. The next step would be to practice on wet grass or a sliding mat. Ensure the players wear the appropriate gear, i.e. baseball pants and sliding pants. They are inexpensive and prevent a great deal of pain.

    d. Make sure the runners glide into the slide, don't let them drop or fall into it.

    e. Teach popping up on the bag, when appropriate. This allows the runner to see the situation quicker.

    f. When sliding, teach the runners to keep their hands up and out and their head up.

    g. Never teach headfirst sliding at the Little League level. Many leagues have restrictions on head first sliding. Ask your league officials.

8. *RUNNING TO FIRST*

    After the hit, glance at the first-base coach but don't stare. There are several things the runner is looking to do. They are:

        a. *STAY AT FIRST:* Coach in upright position, both hands up yelling; "Here! Here!" The runner crosses the base by touching the front of the bag and immediately looking right for a missed ball.

        b. *TURN AND LOOK TWO:* Coach points to second base with his right hand while holding his left hand up. Coach yells, "Look two!" Runner turns and locates the ball. Coach helps the player locate the ball by telling the player where the ball is.

        c. *GO TO SECOND OR THIRD*: Coach points to second base with his right hand while making a circle motion with his left. Coach yells, "Go two!" or "Go three!" Once the runner rounds first base they are to immediately pick up the third base coach.

        d. When turning toward second base after a base hit, have the runners run to the right side of the first base line, two thirds the way up the line and start an arcing turn toward second base, hitting the inside corner of the first base bag.

Table 7.17: Runners Turning at First

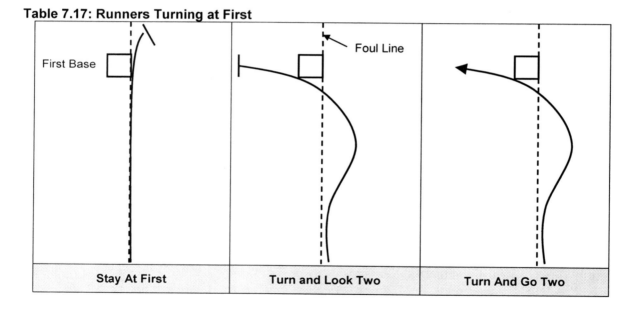

Stay At First	Turn and Look Two	Turn And Go Two

Other things to remember:

    e. Teach the runners to run everything out! Even a standard routine infield play can be dropped.

    f. Don't let the players develop bad habits young.

    g. Be alert and aggressive. One lazy throw or a mental lapse from a fielder can mean an extra bag.

    h. Where appropriate, teach the players to automatically run on a third strike swing and miss. Be relentless on this as a coach. You can use this as a MTM drill. See Section Six on Motivation Through Movement.

    i. Being fast is not the same as being quick. Teach the runners that getting a good jump is more important than being able to run fast. One year my fourth fastest runner had the most steals and set a school record.

Table 7.18: Multi Team Run Drill

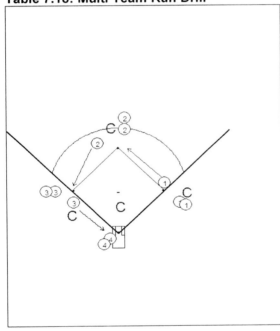

MULTI TEAM RUN DRILL

1. Runner at the plate simulates a swing and moves to First. On the way to first the runner picks up the coach and looks for:

a. "Here!" - Stay at first run through the bag to the right looking right for a past ball. Runner turns right and returns to bag.

b. "Look two!" - Runner make a slight arc to second base touches inside of the bag looking for ball and second base.

c. "Go two!" - Runner runs to second base picking up the third base coach half way.

2. Coach on third can practice hold or go home.

3. Teach primary and secondary leads at each bag.

4. Coach can yell, "Back!" - Teach how to return to each bag.

5. Third base runners teach down foul, back fair.

6. Home plate teach proper sliding techniques.

Table 7.19: Sprint and Walks

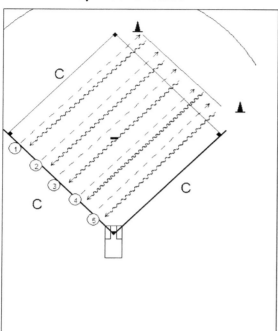

SPRINT AND WALKS

1. Sprint and walks are a good exercise after practice or distance running. They are used to help condition and prepare the player for short bursts used in base running and defense.
2. Set up cones in the infield. Have players sprint to cone and walk back to start point. This is not a timed event.
3. 5 - 25 repetitions are used depending on age and athletic condition.

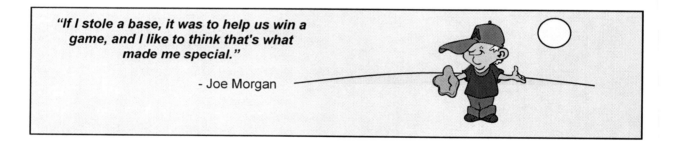

"If I stole a base, it was to help us win a game, and I like to think that's what made me special."

- Joe Morgan

Signs

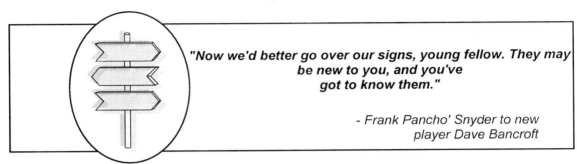

"Now we'd better go over our signs, young fellow. They may be new to you, and you've got to know them."

- Frank Pancho' Snyder to new player Dave Bancroft

Signs are an important element of the game. They allow the coach to secretly communicate with the players on the field. Signs can include, but are not limited to, defensive, offensive, and catching and pitching signs. I would recommend you introduce signs to your Little League players, but I would suggest you keep them simple.

1. *OFFENSIVE SIGNS*
Here are some easy to remember offensive signs.

     a. Bunt – Belt ("B" belt, "B" bunt)
     b. Steal – Shirt ("S" shirt, "S" steal)
     c. Hit and Run – Hat ("H" hat, "H" hit and run)

Other signs appropriate for this age group are the indicator, the "I got it coach" sign, and the "re-do" sign.

     a. INDICATOR: The indicator precedes the actual sign. It is used to alert the batter of an up-coming signal. It is also used to confuse the opponents. The bunt, steal, or hit and run sign, usually follows immediately after the indicator. Common indicators include touching a wrist, elbow or cheek.

     b. I GOT IT COACH: The batter should acknowledge every sign he receives from the coach. Having the players touch the brim of their helmet is a good way to do this.

     c. RE-DO: The player uses the "re-do" sign when they are confused or missed the sign. The "re-do" sign is accomplished by making a small quick circle with the first finger of either hand.

2. *DEFENSIVE SIGNS*

The amount of defensive signs you use is directly proportional to the league in which you coach. For the younger levels I would again recommend you keep things simple. Here are some suggestions.

    a. Practice all your defensive signals and subsequence moves during practice. This allows the players to see what they look like from the field. It is important that everyone understands all the signals.

    b. Appropriate signals at the Little, Junior League, Senior League and middle school levels include:

        1. Positioning the infield and outfield.
        2. First and third situations (Runner on first and third).
        3. Bunt coverage.
        4. Who covers on steals.
        5. Base coverage.
        6. Pick offs.
        7. Type of pitch. Note, this gets more complicated at the more advanced levels and should not be a priority at the Little League and Minor League levels. The key at this level is to throw strikes.

Catching a Pop Fly

"A batter is out on a batted ball, fair or foul, if *caught on the fly or after one bounce."*

- 1858 Rule of Baseball

Many routine pop-fly's at the Little League level are dropped due to confusion. There are simple items to teach to help with this.

a. Teach the players to yell, "Ball!" when they want the ball. Yelling "ball" takes less time than, "I've got it!"

b. Teach everyone that the infielders have priority over the outfielders, but it's the outfielder's responsibility to call off the infielder.

c. Infielders have priority over the pitcher.

d. Pitcher has priority over the catcher in front of the plate.

e. Catcher has everything behind the plate.

f. Call for the ball only when it gets to its peak.

g. Everyone should move on a fly ball, especially with runners on base. Get the outfielders used to backing up the bags and each other. Teach a, "When in doubt, do something!" mentality.

h. Catch the ball out and in front of the body moving in the direction of the throw. For the catchers, this may mean moving out and turning to the ball (See section on catchers).

i. Use tennis balls to start the training. A tennis ball to the head will not hurt the players and it builds confidence.

j. In the outfield, have the players use a drop step to move back to the ball versus drifting to the ball. A ball hit behind and to the player's right starts with the player stepping back with the right foot and running to the spot the ball is expected to drop. Drifting typically occurs when a player steps backwards toward a ball hit over their head.

Table 7.20: Pop Fly Coverage

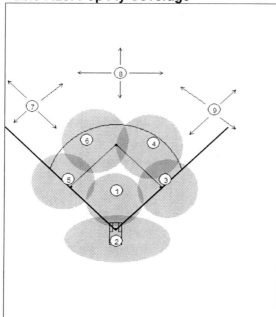

BASIC POP FLY COVERAGE

Things to remember:

1. Infielder has priority over the outfielders, but it's the outfielder's job to call the infielder off.
2. Infielder has priority over the pitcher.
3. Pitcher has priority over the catcher in front of the plate.
4. Call for the ball only when it reaches its peak.
5. Yell "Ball!" It's easier than yelling, "I got it!"
6. Keep the assignments simple.

Table 7.21: Pop Fly Drill

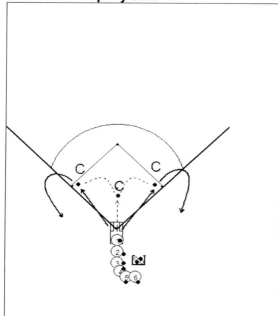

POP FLY DRILL

1. Players toss the coach a ball and runs up the first or third base line.
2. Players open up to the coach looking for the fly ball.
3. Coach tosses ball ahead of runner.
4. Make sure players catch ball over their shoulders and never turn away from the ball.
5. Alternate sides.
6. Great gym drill.

Cut-Off's

Cut-off's can be confusing and there are many different types of cut-off situations. This is compounded by the fact that cut-offs are different than relays. At the Little League level keep the responsibilities simple. Start with the second baseman and shortstop for throws from the outfield. The first baseman can be used as the cut-off for throws home. Initially, I would recommend very limited situational training. Several items to keep in mind when teaching cut-offs are:

a. A cut-off for an outfield throw should be positioned approximately half way between the target and the ball.
b. Have the cut-off shout, "Hit me! Hit me!" With both hands extended up. This allows the fielder to use the sense of hearing and sight to pick up the target quicker.
c. Have the player open up once the ball is on its way by having the player's throwing side point slightly toward the ball. This allows the player to transition to the throw quickly. The 3-Man relay drill is a great teaching aid here. It shows the players how to position themselves to transition the throw quickly. Remember to always have the cut offs turn to the glove side.
d. The player covering the bag should line up the cut-off man, by yelling "Right" or "Left," "In" or "Out."
e. At this level the player covering the bag should call the cut by either yelling, "Let it go" or "Cut." If the ball is cut, train the cut-off man to turn toward the play and run the ball into the infield quickly. See appendix for actual player movement and positions.

Table 7.22: Cut Offs

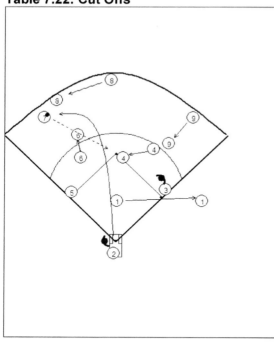

CUT OFF'S (Man on first, fly ball to left field)

The key with teaching cut offs and backing up is getting the players to move on contact. Do not be too concerned if the player misses an assignment as long as they move.

At the Little League level keep the assignments easy. The following would be considered good coverage at this level.

1. 6 moves to cut the ball.
2. 4 moves to cover second base and locates the cut off by telling cut-off to move "right," "left," "in," or "out".
3. 8 moves to left field to back up 7.
4. 9 moves to cover between first base and second base.
5. 1 covers for the bad throw to second or first.
6. Cut off man should be giving a "big" target with raised arms and be yelling, "hit me!"

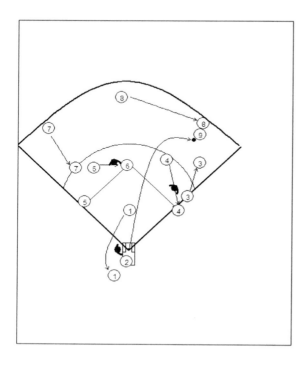

CUT OFF'S (Man on first and second, hit to right field)

1. 8 backs up 9.
2. 3 moves out for the cut.
3. 4 moves to cover first base.
4. 6 moves top cover second base.
5. 5 stays at third.
6. 7 moves to shortstop area to back up throw to second or third.
7. 1 backs up plate.
8. Cut off man should be giving a "big" target with raised arms and be yelling, "hit me!"

Note: You should adjust the above assignments based on the skill level of your individual players. Another variation of the above has 4 move out for the cut off while 3 holds at first base.

Pitching

"Good pitching always stops good hitting..."

- Casey Stengal

Sandy Kofax once said, "I became a better pitcher when I stopped pitching trying to get the batters to miss, and started pitching to get them to swing." This is great advice for the Little Leaguer. Teach the players that the most important pitch in baseball is the first strike.

It is impossible to do the art of pitching any justice in such a short book. Each coach should seek out individual lessons, read training manuals, or view instructional tapes before you attempt to train. Local high school coaches are a great resource. In an attempt to provide some information I will offer this. I once had the privilege of meeting Sam Ellis. Sam was a long time Major League pitching coach for the Cincinnati Reds and other major league teams. He told me there are four absolutes of pitching. They are:

Stay tall
Get back
Stay together
Move downhill

While great advise for older players it may be too general for the younger players to understand. When breaking Sam's four Key Elements down so a ten or an eleven-year-old can understand it, I use the following steps:

1. Throwing foot set.
2. Glove foot set.
3. Establish balance.
4. Glove up.
5. Power breath.
6. Glove foot step back.
7. Throwing foot rotate.
8. Glove knee up - body pivot.
9. Fall forward.
10. Butterfly and foot plant.
11. Rotate and throw.
12. Finish and defend.

1. THE MOUND

Before I explain the above twelve steps, it is essential that young pitchers understand what the mound should look like before they begin to pitch. Too often young pitchers go to the mound with a three or four inch hole in the front of the rubber and they are reluctant to fix it. They end up fighting through the inning with the hole becoming an impediment to good form. While every pitcher is comfortable with something slightly different, there are several rules of thumb they should understand.

    a. Fix the mound every inning before the pitcher begins to pitch.

    b. Establish what is comfortable before the game and maintain it during the game. Even though the Little League has specific requirements for the pitching mound, every rubber and mound is slightly different.

    c. Make sure there is no hole in front of the rubber and the dirt transitions smoothly to the front of the mound. Also fill and smooth the hole created by the throwing foot after the throwing rotation is complete.

    d. The difference between the top of the rubber and the ground in front of the rubber should be no more than two inches.

Table 7.23: Mound Management Diagram

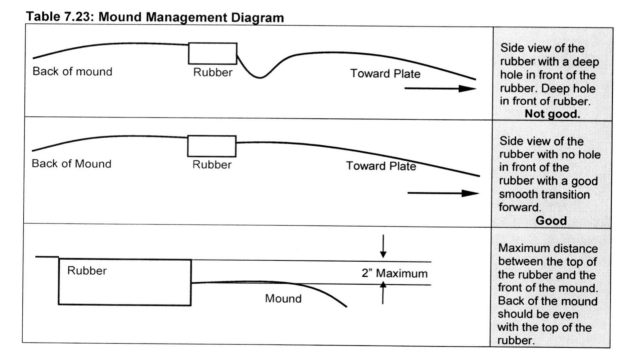

    e. It is extremely helpful to bring the pitchers to the mound during a practice and demonstrate to them how to properly fix it, and how to establish what is comfortable for them. I always have a rake with me and have the pitchers fix their own mound after practice.

2.   *TWELVE STEP PITCHING*

Establishing a good and consistent pre-pitch routine is essential to good pitching. The first step is to have the pitcher relaxed before they set up on the rubber. Don't allow them become too anxious to pitch the ball. Having them become methodical in what they do helps them to relax and sequence their routines properly.

Step One - *THROWING FOOT SET*

Step one is to establish the throwing foot on the rubber with the ball of the foot slightly over the front of the rubber.

Step Two - *GLOVE FOOT SET*

Once the throwing foot is set the glove foot is brought up and set several inches from the throwing foot and several inches back.

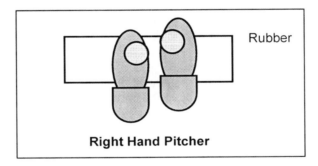

Step Three - *ESTABLISH BALANCE*

A good start to insuring good balance is to have the ball of the throwing foot slightly over the front of the rubber and the ball of the glove foot in the middle of the rubber. Have the pitcher bounce on the balls of his feet. He should be able to maintain good balance.

Step Four - *GLOVE UP*

The glove comes up with the back of the glove pointing to the catcher, lower arm somewhat perpendicular to the ground. Some pitchers like the top of the glove just below their eyes, while others like the top of the glove at their chin. The key is to establish a place where they are most comfortable. The ball is in the glove with the throwing hand on the ball establishing the grip.

Step Five - *POWER BREATH*

Once the hands and feet are set, the pitcher takes a deep breath before starting the pitching sequence. For older pitchers receiving signals from the catcher I recommend a power breath before the signals and a less conspicuous breath after receiving the signals. Two power breaths, one before the signals and one after the signal may give the other team an advantage when men are on base.

Step Six - *GLOVE FOOT STEP BACK*

For a right-handed pitcher, the pitcher steps back to the left and back a few inches at a forty-five degree angle. The key during the step back is to minimize head movement and maintain good balance. A step too far back will pull the pitcher off balance. The body should not rock back. More than a four to six-inch step at the Little League will usually result in a balance problem.

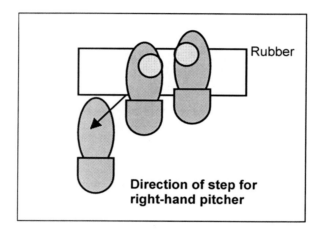

Step Seven – *THROWING FOOT ROTATE*

For a right-handed pitcher, weight is shifted to the ball of the back foot and the right foot is lifted slightly, rotated and placed in front of the rubber. It is important to have the pitcher stay tall during this transition.

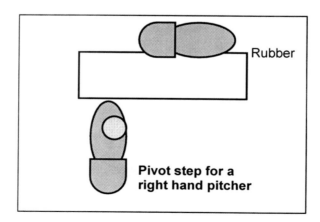

Step Eight - *GLOVE KNEE UP, BODY PIVOT*

As the weight is shifted back to the front foot, the throwing knee is brought up belt high as the body rotates ninety degrees to the plate. The pitcher should be able to maintain balance for ten seconds in this position. Getting the pitchers into this position during practice and having hem hold the position for ten seconds is a great balance drill.

Step Nine - *FALL FORWARD*

The move to the plate starts with a slight shift in weight down hill. Unchecked the player will fall forward. This is natural.

Step Ten - *BUTTERFLY AND FOOT PLANT*

As the body begins to move forward the arms come apart in a butterfly motion. Back of the glove points to the target, throwing arm straight back fingers on top. Arms form a straight line to the target. This is important, as the typical Little League pitcher will tend to throw with arms bent, their elbow down and their hand under the ball.

At the same time the pitcher's weight moves forward and the arms butterfly, the front foot slides forward and gets planted out front with the toe pointing home.

Table 7.24: Slide Step Forward

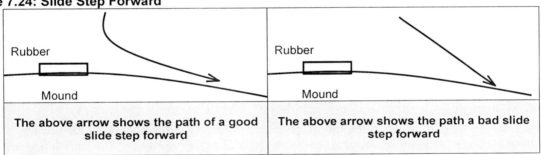

Rubber	Rubber
Mound	Mound
The above arrow shows the path of a good slide step forward	The above arrow shows the path a bad slide step forward

Step Eleven - *ROTATE AND THROW*

Once the front foot is planted the throw begins. There are different opinions as to what rotates first. Some say the upper body while others say the hips. At the Little League level I would recommend not spending too much time on this as long as the pitcher finishes well.

As the pitcher rotates, teach the pitchers to keep their elbows up with the upper arm parallel to the ground. Different arm angles can be taught when they are older. A good start has the upper arm, lower arm and wrist at ninety-degree angles to each other in the middle of the throw.

Step Twelve - *FINISH AND DEFEND*

There are several musts for proper rotation and a good finish. They are:

    a. Throwing hand cuts across the body and finishes in the opposite pocket.

b. The glove is tucked under the glove-side armpit. This is taught by having the tip of the glove pointing home bringing the tip of the glove to the armpit.

c. The throwing foot is rotated so that it lands slightly out in front of the plant foot.

d. Head is up looking at the target.

e. Once the rotation is complete the hands come out, palms to the ball ready to defend.

3. *PITCH COUNT (ARM SAFETY)*

This is a heavily debated topic. The Little League has developed guidelines that limit the amount of games a pitcher can pitch in an attempt to protect players. Coaches sometimes get carried away with pitch count by either becoming too obsessive with it or oblivious to it. Factors that should be considered when trying to determine reasonable pitch count include:

a. *PLAYER SIZE*: Bigger players may have more strength than smaller players. This is not to say small players cannot be effective pitchers. My smallest, starting pitcher during one of my high school seasons was my best pitcher and could outlast all the other pitchers on the roster.

b. *PLAYER STENGTH:* Some players are simply stronger than others. Children develop at different rates and coaches should be aware that just because a pitcher may be the oldest player on the team, it doesn't necessarily mean he can pitch more.

c. *PLAYER TALENT LEVEL:* Some players are genetically better pitchers than others. They possess natural talent that allows them to be more effective on the mound.

d. *PLAYER AGE AND EXPERIENCE:* Typically, experienced pitchers are able to last longer than beginners. The only word of caution I will offer here is that just because a pitcher has more experience, it does not necessarily mean they have been trained properly. An improperly trained, experienced pitcher can develop as many problems as a novice.

e. *PITCH COUNT:* The following is a table that I would suggest for the different age groups. I suggest the following as a guideline only:

Table 7.25: Pitch Count

Age (Years)	League	Suggested Maximum Pitches Per Game	Suggested Maximum Games Per Week
8-10	Minor League	50	2
11-12	Little League	60	2
12-14	Little League, Junior League, Middle School	80	2
14-16	Senior League, High School (JV), Junior Legion	100	3 - With at least one day in between games

    f. *PITCHING PLAN:* A great way of avoiding injury is to establish a weekly, pitching plan. The pitching plan is made a week in advance and is used as a guide. They are typically adjusted based on factors such as weather, injuries and availability. The one I use is simple and looks like the following:

Table 7.26: Pitching Plan

Day (Date)	Versus	Starter	Reliever	Closer
Monday	**Smithfield**	*Bobby*	*Frank*	*Jon*
Tuesday	**Woodstock**	*Ted*	*Bruce*	*Tommy*
Wednesday	**South East**	*Frank*	*Jon*	*Frank*
Thursday	**Palmer**	*Bobby*	*Don*	*Neal*
Friday	**North Side**	*Ted*	*Bruce*	*Tommy*
Saturday	**Franklin**	*Jon*	*Frank*	*Mitch*
Sunday	**Lincoln**	*Neal*	*Ted*	*Tommy*

    g. *DOUBLE DUTY:* It is not unusual for players to be playing in two leagues simultaneously. A typical situation would be a player playing Little League and middle school, or a player playing Senior League and high school. I strongly suggest that you speak with the other coach to avoid pitchers pulling double duty. My rule of thumb is school teams take priority over Little League. The important thing is to establish a plan with the other coach.

    h. *DAILY THROWING:* I developed a plan that has our pitchers throwing each day (Unless their arms are hurting), limiting the number of throws, and the speed in which they throw depending on their game-time activity. The best way to develop a young arm is to have the pitchers throw properly everyday.

    i. *WARM-UPS:* Insure the pitcher has plenty of time to warm up prior to a game. I limit the speed in which they throw slowly building to about seventy-five percent of their maximum throwing speed. There's an old baseball adage about warming up, "Don't let your pitchers throw all their best pitches in the bullpen."

"Anybody's best pitch is the one the batters ain't hitting that day."

- Christy Mathewson

The Catcher

"*Catching is much like managing: managers don't really win games, but they can lose plenty of them. The same way with catching. If you're doing a quality job you should be almost anonymous.*"

- Bob Boone

Catching has presented several different challenges for me over the years. I had several seasons where everyone wanted to be the catcher. I also had seasons where nobody wanted the job. As with every other position on the team, I would suggest that you give every player a chance to experience the position. As your season progresses however, you may have to settle on several players that are able to play the position effectively.

1.   THE FIELD GENERAL

If pitching is the most important position on the field, catching is the toughest. Being a catcher is not for the weak of heart. Good catchers must possess:

        a.   Above average courage.
        b.   Good field and game awareness.
        c.   High amount of confidence.
        d.   High level of energy.
        e.   Good intelligence.
        f.   Good mental and physical toughness.

The catcher also needs to be, what I call, a good "Field General." They are always the loudest and most enthusiastic player on the field. The catcher's job is to constantly keep the team aware of defensive game situations. This includes constantly making the team aware of the number of outs, where the next play is, who's backing up whom, etc. If there is a full-time cheerleader on the team, the catcher is it!

2.   CATCHING EQUIPMENT

Catching equipment comes in different types and sizes. Make sure the equipment is properly fitted to the player. Properly fitted equipment does not move or flop around when the catcher runs or throws. I always try to have two sets of equipment available to accommodate different size players on the team. I also pre-fit each potential catcher with a set before each game. Don't be caught dealing with fitting equipment during the game, it is time consuming and short cuts are always taken. Proper equipment includes:

a. Mask with throat guard.
b. Chest protector.
c. Shin guards.
d. Cup (on male players).
e. Helmet (or hockey style mask).
f. Catcher's mitt.

3. BLOCKING THE BALL

Blocking a ball in the dirt is a game making, or game breaking skill for a catcher. A game can be easily lost if a catcher has trouble blocking a ball in the dirt. More important than the loss of a game, is the frustration the catcher develops feeling he/she is losing the game single handedly. When training catchers, make sure they understand what they are responsible for, and what they are not responsible for.

In order to keep it simple I tell my Little League catchers they are responsible for every ball they can reach, a passed ball. The pitcher is responsible for every ball they cannot reach, a wild pitch. When blocking a ball the catcher's primary mission is to keep the ball in front of him/her. Teach this by:

a. Having catchers slide their entire body laterally to the ball, keeping the center of their body centered on the ball. The catcher's chest remains squared to the field. Ensure that they do not turn their body to the side or attempt a one-handed catch. A good drill for this is to have one coach toss a ball in the dirt to the right or left of the catcher, while another coach slightly pushes the catcher by his or her shoulders to the ball.
b. Have the catcher keep his or her chin down against the chest. It is safer for the catcher and a deflected ball off a catcher's mask facing down will typically deflect forward. A ball deflected off a mask turned away, will usually deflect to the side or behind the catcher. A good way to help catchers get used to this is to use tennis balls easily tossed off the mask.
c. Having the catcher keep his or her knees down on the ground with the glove covering the hole between the knees.
d. Shoulders are turned in creating a bowl like upper body.
e. Teach the catchers with runners on, they should always locate the ball first, and the runners second.

4. FLY BALL BEHIND THE PLATE

Locating, moving to, and catching a pop fly behind the plate is a very difficult task. Coaches should teach the following to make it as easy as possible.

a. First, train your pitchers to point to the ball while in the air. They see it before the catcher. This gives the catcher a general idea where the ball is, making it easier for them to locate.

b. The mask comes off with the throwing hand. The catcher grabs the bottom of the mask and removes it by flipping it up and over the head.

c. Once the ball is located the catcher throws the mask to the ground away from the play.

d. Have the catcher face the fly ball when possible. This means they must get to the spot they expect the ball to fall and turn toward the ball. It is easier catching a ball coming to you versus a ball moving away from you.

5. *PICKING OFF A RUNNER*

The ability of a catcher to pick off a runner stealing a base can take different forms with young players. The best way to throw a runner out attempting to steal a bag is for the catcher to start with a quick diagonal shuffle step with the throwing foot behind. This is accomplished while the catcher stands. Older catchers may be able to reach the bag using this method. Younger catchers however, may not be strong enough and will have to take a "wind-up" step to generate enough power to get the ball to the bag.

At the Little League level your primary mission is to teach catchers the most efficient way for them to get the ball to the bag. You can help them accomplish this by making sure their mask and other equipment is fitted tightly, and they learn how to properly throw a ball. It's the catcher's job to get the ball to the bag and the infielder's job to catch the ball and make the tag. A perfect throw arrives at the bag at the same time as the fielder; knee high, on the runner's side of the bag.

Run Downs

While run downs do not happen every game, Little Leaguers should be taught how to handle them and what their specific responsibilities are. Again, the key with Little League is to keep the assignments simple. Run down assignments become more complicated at the higher levels, but for now get them used to doing the basics. Several keys in teaching how to properly handle a run down are:

a. Every player is involved in the play.
b. The first goal is to run the player back to the bag they came from.
c. The second objective is to get the out.
d. Try to make only one throw.
e. Hold the ball high so the fielder receiving the throw can see it.
f. The fielder with the ball runs at the runner with the ball in hand.
g. Never fake a throw; it usually results only in faking out the fielders.
h. The fielder expecting the throw presents a good target with their glove up and out, palm of the glove facing the ball.
i. The fielder expecting the throw communicates to the player with the ball by yelling, "Now!" when the fielder wants the ball.
j. Timing the throw is important and should always occur in the same direction the runner is running.
k. Always cover two bags ahead of the runner.
l. Rotate out after a throw.

The objective is again to make one throw, but many times, especially at the younger levels, more throws are necessary to get the out or to force the runner back to the bag they came from. To help with this, I have the fielders rotate to the far side of the run down and move in behind the line backing up the throw or covering the bag. They do this by rotating to the outside of the play. The outside of the play is the opposite side of the throw coming at them. The small black circle below shows this.

Table 7:27: Run Down Rotation

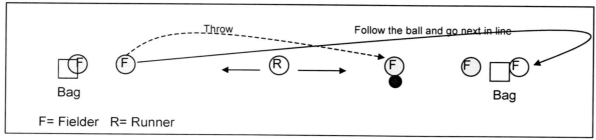

Bag   Bag

F= Fielder R= Runner

Table 7.28: Run Downs

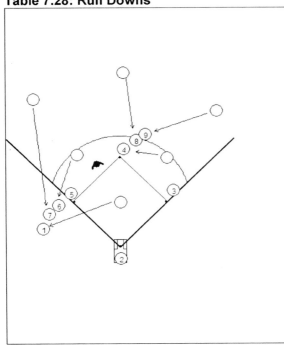

RUN DOWN (Second to Third)

1. Every player is in the play.
2. First goal is to run the runner back to the bag; second goal is to get the out.
3. Make only one throw.
4. Throw with the throwing hand up, presenting the ball to your teammate.
5. Don't fake a throw. This usually results in faking out your teammate.
6. Communicate! The player that wants the ball yells, "Now!" when they want the ball.
7. Always cover two bags ahead of the runner.
8. Follow the direction of the throw and rotate to the back of the far line moving to the right.
9. Next player in line covers the bag and anticipates the tag.

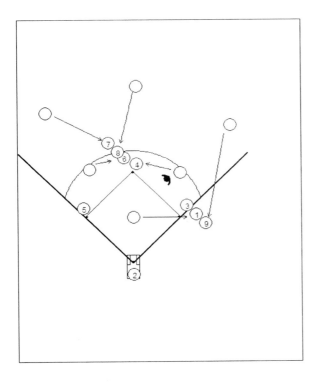

RUN DOWN (First to Second)

1. Same as above.
2. It is recommended that the catcher holds and covers the plate at the Little League level.

Game Time

"Youngsters of Little League can survive under-coaching a lot better than over-coaching."

- Willie Mays
Hall of Famer

The most effective way to get the most out of each game is to be prepared and organized. Each coach should have assigned responsibilities, prior to the game.

1. PRE-GAME

    a. Have the players arrive ready to play 30-40 minutes before game time.

    b. Have the players stretch and warm up before the game. This is usually done in the outfield and can be managed by team captains.

    c. Establish a warm up and throwing routine before the first game. Practice this before your season starts. You can develop a great deal of game-time confidence during your pre-game warm ups.

    d. Establish how infield practice will be conducted at practice before the first game. I practice this often. It only takes a few minutes and the players play better when they look good in the pre-game warm ups.

    e. In Little League, pre-game batting practice is usually shared with both teams. Rotate players in from each team.

    f. Use buckets to facilitate batting practice.

    g. Shake hands with the opposing coach and the umpires.

2. DURING THE GAME

    a. Stay organized. Have only one coach in charge of the scorebook and constantly let the players know who's batting next and who's playing where.

    b. Inform players of substitutions at least a half inning before they are made. This allows the players to get mentally prepared.

    c. Have players cheer for teammates.

3. POST GAME

    a. You and the team shake hands with everyone after the game. It is, "How you play the game" that's important.

b. Meet with the team immediately after the game away from the parents and review what went well and the improvement opportunities. Say something positive about every player. Ask the other coaches if they have any (positive) input from the game.

c. Give the players something to work on before the next practice.

d. Above all, be positive.

e. Meet briefly with your assistant coaches after the team meeting and compare notes on improvement opportunities for the next practice.

"Baseball is a simple game. If you have good players and if you keep them in the right frame of mind then the manager is a success."

- Sparky Anderson

Section 8. The Post Season

Post Season

For most coaches, the season does not end with the last game. Two year-end items that I feel warrant attention are, the year-end banquet and post-season coach's' evaluation.

1.   *YEAR-END BANQUET*

Most leagues conduct a year-end awards banquet and coaches are usually expected to say a few words. Done properly, it can be a great ending to a great season. Done poorly, it can be an event that leaves players and parents shaking their heads.

Many coaches dread this part of the season. Speaking in public is not an easy thing to do. The key to being successful is to be prepared. Write down what you want to say. Practice it in front of a mirror, and say it over and over again. The more you practice, the more comfortable you'll be when the big day arrives.

The year-end awards banquet can have as much an impact on the future memories of the players as the entire season. Many coaches make the mistake of finishing the season on a sour note, usually because they try to do the right thing, the wrong way. Here are several items to keep in mind as you prepare for your year-end sports banquet or final team get-together.

1. Leave all the problems you had during the season at the field. What's done is done.
2. Say something positive about every player. Don't leave anyone out.
3. Avoid backhanded compliments. Use statements like, "Bobby was one of the hardest workers we had this season and he helped set a great example for the team," versus, "Bobby didn't play well this year, but he sure tried hard."
4. Avoid all attempts to tell jokes about your players; their families often fail to see the humor.
5. Be familiar with the correct pronunciation of all names. There's nothing worse than using a player's name incorrectly, especially after coaching him or her for an entire season.
6. Make sure you thank everyone that was involved including coaches, team moms or dads, and managers.
7. Keep your comments brief and succinct. Avoid all attempts at adlibbing.
8. Picking awards is difficult. The key here is use facts and numbers whenever possible i.e. batting average, RBI's, errors, slugging percentage, steals, etc. I try to avoid awards such as *Most Valuable Player* and *Most Improved Player*, unless there is one person who clearly stands out above all other players. Baseball is a team sport and needs to be played as such in order to be successful. One of your bullpen players could be the most valuable player even though he or she didn't have the best batting average. The point is, it is difficult to determine who the most valuable player is. A good way to test this

is to ask, "Would everyone on the team and their parents agree with my choice?" If not, I would suggest the following:

    a.   Substitute *Outstanding Player Award* for *Most Valuable*.

    b.   Substitute *Coaches' Award* for *Most Improved Player*.

Remember

No matter what your outcome or your team record, finish the season on a positive note.

2. *POST SEASON COACHES' EVALUATIONS*

Many research and educational experts define evaluation as the process of determining the effectiveness, merit, or quality of a program. I agree with this definition and welcome evaluation as a great way to identify improvement opportunities.

There are several sources of meaningful evaluation available to youth basketball coaches. They can include:

    a. The person you report to. This can be an athletic director, town recreation manager, or league official.

    b. Other coaches.

    c. Experts such as college or professional coaches.

    d. Players.

    e. Parents.

A key with evaluations, is to view them for what they are, someone's opinion on how they viewed your performance as a coach. A great saying my grandmother used often was:

> ## "You are what people perceive you to be, not what you perceive yourself as."

While I do not agree this statement applies to all aspects of our lives, it may have some application in coaching. A large disconnect can exist if we view ourselves as good coaches, while those around us, especially our players, think otherwise. Players, no matter how young can provide very insightful opinions about our abilities. The trick is to first, get their opinions in an orderly fashion, and then second, learn from them. At the beginning of this book I use the quote, "The measure of a good coach is not how well he knows the game, it's how well he can teach it." Keep this in mind as you learn.

The following is an example of an evaluation I use with parents, players and coaching associates. It has helped me recognize my weaknesses and strengths. I also have a year-end team meeting in which I allow the players to speak freely about the season and what they feel can be improved upon for the next season. Both have been extremely helpful in my quest to become a better coach.

129

Table 8.1: Coach's Evaluation

PATTERSON SPORTS
Coach's Post-Season Evaluation

Coach's Name:_____ Date:_____

Team:_____

Instructions: Each player is to carefully read each category and check the appropriate box.

Coach's Knowledge of the Game	The coach exhibits an in-depth knowledge of the game and how to teach the required skills. ☐	The coach exhibits a working knowledge of the game and how to teach the required skills. ☐	The coach has a less than adequate knowledge of the game and has difficulty teaching drills and skills. ☐	The coach does not know the game and he/she does not know how to teach the skills and drills. ☐
Coach's Organizational Skills	Coach is highly organized. No time is wasted at practices and games. ☐	Coach is mostly prepared. Little time is wasted at practices and games. ☐	Coach often unprepared for practices and games. Practice time often wasted. ☐	Coach is never prepared for practice or games. Practice time always wasted. ☐
Coach's Ability to Teach the Game	Coach is able to break skills down and explain well ☐	Coach is able to break most skill down and explain. Has some difficulty with several skills ☐	Coach is not able to break most skills down. Usually has a difficult time making players understand. ☐	Coach is difficult to understand or has little ability to teach ☐
Coach's Ability To Affect the Players Enthusiasm and Motivation	Coach is highly motivated and made the season extremely enjoyable. ☐	Coach motivated players. Season mostly enjoyable. ☐	Coach motivated players at times. Season was not always enjoyable. ☐	Coach did little to motivate players. Not an enjoyable season. ☐
Coach's Ability to Manage Games.	Coach does an excellent job managing games and gets the most from the team every game. ☐	Coach does a good job managing games. ☐	Coach does a less than fair job managing games. Poor game time management lost several games. ☐	Coach did a poor job managing games. Lost many games due to poor game time management. ☐

Coach's Ability to Set an Example	Coach sets a great example for players. ☐	Coach sets a good example for the players most of the time. ☐	Coach seldom sets a good example for the players. ☐	Coach never sets a good example for the players. ☐
Coach's Retainability	Coach should be retained. No changes needed. ☐	Coach should be retained with some additional training. ☐	Coach should be retained. Significant training required. ☐	Coach should not be retained. ☐
Mentorship / Role Model	Coach is an excellent mentor and a great role model for players. ☐	Coach is an OK mentor and, someone the players occasionally look up to. ☐	Coach is not always a good role model and is someone players do not always consider a good role model. ☐	Coach was not a good mentor or role model. ☐

List three items we did well this year:

List three items we did not do well this year:

Comments (Use back of page for additional space):

3. *COLLECTING THE UNIFORMS AND EQUIPMENT*

Collecting uniforms and equipment at the end of the season can be a real headache for a coach. There are two easy ways to do this. The first way is to establish a specific area and time a few minutes before the start of the year-end banquet. Have the players bring their uniforms to the banquet and have a team mom or dad help organize. I found there is usually moms or dads who are much better at coordinating this effort than me. The second way is to have a one-hour pizza party at the end of the season. I also use this time to allow the players a few minutes to evaluate the coaches' performance and offer improvement opportunities for the next season.

Section 9. Appendices

"KEEPING IT FUN"
Little League Baseball and Softball Tips for Conflict Resolution
(Reprinted with permission from Little League Baseball)

In all aspects of life, conflict will arise. So it's not surprising that conflicts would occasionally arise during a Little League season. To help with potential disputes, Little League offers these *six simple steps to conflict resolution.* While these steps may not be applicable to every situation, these basic conflict resolution skills should prove to be helpful in many situations.

Step 1: Speak to the Person in Private
Choose an appropriate time and place.
Never berate a person in public.

Step 2: Listen Actively
Listen fully to the concern.
Ask questions to clarify a point.

Step 3: Repeat Step 1 With Roles Reversed
Identify the person's problem, as you understand it.
Tell you side of the story. Described WHAT happened, not WHY it happened.
Use "I" statements.
Acknowledge their points of view and feelings.

Step 4: Expressing Feelings
Take turns expressing how you feel about the situation.

Step 5: Solving the Problem
Suggest ways to resolve the situation.

Step 6: Select a Win/Win solution.

Find a way to resolve the problem together that benefits you both.

Step 7: Agree on a Follow-up
Offer to meet again if the concern persists

"Seek first to understand, the to be understood"

- Steve Covey, author of *Seven Habits of Highly Effective People*

DISPUTE: A verbal controversy between two or more people, a dispute is not yet a conflict.

CONFLICT: is a state of disagreement and disharmony.

LISTEN ACTIVELY: involves focusing entirely on what the other person is saying, and confirms understanding of both the content of the message and the emotions and feelings underlying the message. For example you can begin the conversation with: ""First help me understand your concerns regarding your son," or later clarify the concern by asking, "So you view speed as your son's best quality on the field and you are upset because you feel I am not utilizing that strength?"

FEELING WORDS: An important aspect of effective communication. Instead of stating opinions, describe how the situation or dispute makes you feel. For example, say something like: "I get angry when you insult my coaching in front of others, because I know I am trying my bet to help the kids.

OTHER SUGGESTIONS:

At the Beginning of the Year:
Send a letter home to the parents establishing the rules in which you would like to run the team. (A copy is available in the back of the Little League Coaches' Clinic Manual) This will set the tone for the year.

Give the players a letter establishing team rules, team philosophy, and team goals.

During the Year:
Never avoid a parent that wants to see you. Always consider their input. Sleep on what they tell you before you form an opinion.

Always talk to an upset parent after the game or practice and never in front of the kids.

Never discuss "why Tim is playing and not your son." Keep that discussion to "This is what your son needs to do in order to play more."

Never yell *AT* a player! Never embarrass a player in front of their peers.

FEEL, FELT, FOUND method: "I know how you feel I felt the same way when my daughter was in the same situation but what I found was that after I really looked at all the possibilities the coach made the right decision".

REMEMBER ABOVE ALL ELSE the game is for them NOT you!

Who's on First: Clueless Coaches

Youth Leagues Need Managers, But Few Parents Know How; Four Strikes, You're Out!
By Sam Walker
Staff Reporter of THE WALL STREET JOURNAL
24 March 2000
(Reprinted with permission from the Wall Street Journal)

AS CHIEF EXECUTIVE of a Washington Internet start-up called SpeakOut.com, Ron Howard cuts a powerful figure in the technology business. But that didn't help him much when he took on his new job: head coach of the Orioles, his son's first-grade baseball Team.

With no coaching experience, Mr. Howard arrived at Norwood Park in Potomac, MD, with a crude practice plan and a list of talking points. Almost immediately, his players staring at the clouds, kicking dirt on one another and asking him whether he'd ever played in the major leagues. Then came the ultimate rebellion: The entire team darted on to the field while he was still talking. "That was the last day I brought a whistle," Mr. Howard says.

If you've ever flirted with the idea of coaching your kids in anything from soccer to inline hockey, you're in luck. From Connecticut to California, organized youth sports programs are bursting at the seams, almost doubling in the past seven years by one estimate and creating a steep demand for new coaches. According to the National Alliance for Youth Sports, the total number of volunteer coaches this year could top three million.

The only problem: A hefty percentage of these folks are completely unqualified. Many haven't put on a pair of cleats in 20 years a have zero experience-teaching children. In sports like soccer, some haven't even seen a game on TV, let alone booted a ball around. It's getting so bad that many leagues are starting to require coaches to attend training clinics. "It used to be that somebody would just hand you a clip board," says Fred Engh, president of NAYS, in West Palm Beach, Fla. "Now you're expect to know something".

Indeed, a whole industry has sprung up to teach fledging coaches, and about 200,000 coaches are trained every year. In San Mateo, Calif., Little League coaches have to attend five meetings and classes during the year umpires at least two games, and soon- if some league officials have their way- pass a comprehensive quiz. Even coaches in more lax programs are running out of excuses for cluelessness. New instructional books are coming out every year, and at least four new Internet coaching sites have popped up, with tips on everything from badminton to lacrosse.

But for some novices, all the training in the world doesn't make a difference, especially when it comes to imported sports such as soccer. "I never played in my life," says Harry Glazer, a technology lawyer from Great Falls, VA.

His introduction to soccer coaching went something like this: After watching his players run amok for a few minutes, Mr. Glazer decided to drop his practice plan and resort to the only trick he could think of to restore order: teaching his kids to do the Macarena. "It was insanity," he says. "I felt like a substitute teacher."

Even now even after several years of coaching, Mr. Glazer says he still botches substitutions and often defers to kids who know more about the game than he does. Chief among them: his son, Louis, who weighs in n everything from choosing team mascots to picking team colors to drafting players. "I don't get to goof off a lot," says the nine-year-old.

Not that new coaches who've played sports always fare better. Charlie Santos-Buch, a New York Financier who runs the Little League program in Darien, Ct. says he'll never forget one first-time coach who showed impressive form whacking line drives to the outfield. The only problem was that his players were only six years old. "It was funny until the kids started getting pelted in the head," he says.

Enrollment Up

According to American Sports Data Inc. of Hartsdale N.Y., adults are about 50% more likely to encourage their children to participate in sports than they were 10 years ago. Combine that with favorable demographics and wild growth in girl's sports, and you've got a ballooning market for organized leagues. In Darien alone, Little League enrollment has nearly doubled in five years to 1300 kids from 750.

With that kind of growth comes a nearly unquashable demand for coaches, and the rise of a new form of peer pressure in towns across America: the annual youth coach cattle call. In Jupiter Fla., Chuck Yannette says he trotted out all the usual excuses when a youth-league official asked him to coach his daughter's softball team this spring- too busy at work, no experience, only if I'm the last resort. "They called back five minutes later and told me I was the last resort," says the landscape architect. "How could I say no".

It's a decision that Mr. Yannette wasn't totally thrilled with at the end of his first game, which the team lost 15-8. Before the game even started, he had to attend a sportsmanship clinic and watch hours of videos just to learn how to conduct a practice and teach batting. The workload, he says is "like taking night classes at a community college."

But whatever drives them to accept the job, most coaches say the real challenge is absorbing it into work schedules that don't lend themselves to a predictable afternoon clock. The busiest coaches today say they have to take re-eye flights home or buy cellular phones to communicate with parents on the road. Others disguise their coaching duties by scheduling them as "business meetings." Fred Cooper may be vice president of finance at Toll Brothers, a luxury homebuilder, but on summer evenings he's forced to change clothes in his car – on the way to batting practice in Princeton, N.J.

Once there, Mr. Cooper says there's no shortage of other obstacles to deal with: like the time a giant groundhog appeared on the field in the middle of a close game, or when his players wandered off the field to chase butter flies. And he once watched his team bow an 11-run lead when an ice cream truck unexpectedly dropped by. "I considered threatening the driver," he says. For his part, Mr. Cooper's 11-year old son, Erik, has this assessment of his dad's struggles: Sometimes, he says, "I start to feel sorry for him."

Not surprisingly, the average coach's career is short- lived, usually about two to three years. Mr. Howard, the Washington Internet company CEO, only made it through one season. His take on the experience: Running a practice with first-graders is like meeting with 75 corporate investors, with a slight difference. "I made the mistake of treating them like little men, which they're not." He says of the Orioles. "Men you can reason with."

OTHER RESOURCES FOR THE LITTLE LEAGUE COACH

National Alliance for Youth Sports (NAYS)

National Alliance For Youth Sports
2050 Vista Parkway
West Palm Beach, Florida 33411
Phone 561.684.1141
800.688.KIDS
800.729.2057
Fax 561.684-2546
www.nays.org

The National Alliance For Youth Sports (NAYS) is America's leading advocate for positive and safe sports and activities for children. Today, NAYS offers programs and services for everyone involved in youth sports experiences, including professional administrators, volunteer administrators, volunteer coaches, officials, parents and young athletes.

Athletes for a Better World

Athletes for a Better World Headquarters
PO Box 99007
Seattle, WA 98139-0007
Phone: 206-281-2684
Fax: 206-281-2784
www.aforbw.org

American Red Cross

American Red Cross

The American Red Cross offers first aid and CPR training for coaches all over the world. To find your nearest local chapter visit the Red Cross at: www.redcross.org

For Northeast Connecticut contact the Red Cross at:
Tel: 1-860-678-2700
Email: http://charteroak.redcross.org

Jes-Soft

Copyright: 1998-2002 Jes-Soft.
The plays and drills listed in this book were created utilizing
Baseball Playbook Version 0.80, *developed by J.E. Smit.*
Jes-Sports is found at: www.jes-soft.com

Jes Baseball

Little League Baseball and Softball
Little League Eastern Regional
Headquarters
PO Box 2926
Bristol, CT 06011
Telephone: 860-585-4730
Fax: 860-585-4734
Email: eastregion@littleleague.org

America's Game

170 Cross Road
Waterford, CT 06385
Phone: 860- 444-9687
Fax: 860-444-8790
Email: www.americasgame .com

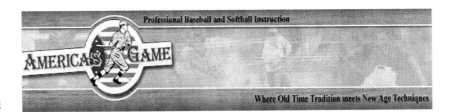

Baseball Almanac

Where What Happened Yesterday is Being Preserved Today

"This site doesn't have any rivals. Every historical information or feat you want on baseball is right here."
  - Sports Collectors Digest (*Top 10 Must See Sites*)

Baseball Almanac can be found at: www.baseball-almanac.com
11400 SW 40th Terrace, Miami, FL 3316

Baseball Fever

A great online discussion forum for baseball enthusiasts of all ages.

Baseball Fever can be found at: www.baseball-fever.com

Patterson Sports
Any questions about coaching Little League contact us at:
107 Providence Street
Putnam, CT 06260
Fax: 1-860-928-5611
Email: pattersonsports@yahoo.com

Hundreds of coaches have found *How to Coach Little League Baseball: A Short East to Follow Guide on How to Begin Your Little League Coaching Career,* a great resource. You can order your copy from Book Locker Inc. at www.**booklocker.com**

"He who dares to teach must never cease to learn!"

- Unknown